THE GEOGRAPHY
OF EXECUTION

THE GEOGRAPHY OF EXECUTION

The Capital Punishment Quagmire in America

KEITH HARRIES
DERRAL CHEATWOOD

ROWMAN & LITTLEFIELD PUBLISHERS, INC.
Lanham • Boulder • New York • London

ROWMAN & LITTLEFIELD PUBLISHERS, INC.

Published in the United States of America
by Rowman & Littlefield Publishers, Inc
4720 Boston Way, Lanham, Maryland 20706

3 Henrietta Street
London WC2E 8LU, England

Copyright © 1997 by Rowman & Littlefield Publishers, Inc.

All rights reserved. No part of this publication may be reproduced, stored in a retrieval system, or transmitted in any form or by any means, electronic, mechanical, photocopying, recording, or otherwise, without the prior permission of the publisher.

British Cataloging in Publication Information Available

Library of Congress Cataloging-in-Publication Data

Harries, Keith D.
    The geography of execution: the capital punishment quagmire in America/Keith Harries, Derral Cheatwood.
        p. cm.
    Includes bibliographical references and index.
    ISBN 0–8476–8156–4 (alk. paper). — ISBN 0–8476–8157–2 (pbk. : alk. paper)
    1. Capital punishment—United States. 2. Violent crimes—United States. I. Cheatwood, Derral. II. Title.
HV8699.U5H37   1997
364.6'6'0973—dc20   96–43347
                                                                                 CIP

ISBN 0–8476–8156–4 (cloth : alk. paper)
ISBN 0–8476–8157–2 (pbk : alk. paper)

Printed in the United States of America

    ∞™ The paper used in this publication meets the minimum requirements of American National Standard for Information Sciences—Permanence of Paper for Printed Library Materials, ANSI Z39. 48-1984.

Contents

Figures	ix
Tables	xi
Acknowledgments	xiii
Chapter 1: The Issue in Context	1
International perspectives	1
Political pressure	3
Opinion polls	7
Capital punishment as a moral decision	10
Theory/deterrence	11
Capital punishment and geography	12
Directions	14
Chapter 2: The Historical Geography of Capital Punishment in America	17
Data sources and method	17
An overview of execution	18
Methods of execution: origin and diffusion	24
Recent trends	29
Homicide and execution	32
Examples of regional complexity: Maryland and neighboring Virginia and the District of Columbia	34
Conclusion	38
Chapter 3: Capital Punishment and State Corrections Systems: Is There an Impending Crisis?	41
The pressure of practical numbers	43
Where are we now?	44
Option 1: executions	46
Option 2: the grim prison of the future	50
Option 3: operations as normal	55
Summary and conclusion	57

Chapter 4: The Geography of Capital Punishment and Homicide:
 Regions of Violence   60

  Precursors   61
  Data base   62
  Research question   62
  Methods   64
  Analysis   65
  Conclusion   68

Chapter 5: Capital Punishment, Race, and Gender   71

  Capital punishment and race   72
  Capital punishment and women   76
  Analysis   79
  Conclusion   88

Chapter 6: Capital Punishment and the Deterrence of Violent
 Crime in Comparable Counties   94

  Review of the question   95
  Sample and methodology   98
  Findings   104
  Conclusion and discussion   107

Chapter 7: The Life-Without-Parole Sanction   109

  The life-without-parole sanction: what is it?   111
  The impact of the life-without-parole sentence on
   the criminal justice system   115
  Is life-without-parole an alternative to life or to death? 119
  Life-without-parole: what we need to know   121
  Legal cases and state codes cited   122

Chapter 8: Epilogue   123

  Business as usual?   123
  Scope for further research   123
  Changes working through the system   124
  Public defender decline   124
  Will the floodgates open?   125
  Persistence of geographic variation   126
  Moral authority   126

Appendix I: Changes in the Espy File Between 1986 and 1995   128

Appendix II: States and Their Methods of Execution	131
Appendix III: Technical Notes	134
References	138
Index	150
About the Authors	155

Figures

1.1.	State executions and status of the death penalty in 1995.	3
1.2.	Attitudes toward the death penalty for persons convicted of murder.	8
1.3.	Percent of college freshmen reporting that capital punishment should be abolished, 1969–94.	9
2.1.	Annual execution frequencies, U.S., 1608–1985.	19
2.2.	Execution frequencies by U.S. counties, Growth Era (to 1879).	20
2.3.	Execution frequencies by U.S. counties, Stability Era, 1880–1929.	21
2.4.	Execution frequencies by U.S. counties, Peak Era, 1930s.	21
2.5.	Execution frequencies by U.S. counties, Decline Era (since 1940).	22
2.6.	Origin and diffusion of electrocution.	26
2.7.	Origin and diffusion of the gas chamber.	27
2.8.	Methods of execution, by states.	28
2.9.	Executions, 8 July 1987, through 27 April 1994.	31
2.10.	Homicide and execution rates, U.S., 1900–1985.	32
3.1.	Three execution plateaus.	42
3.2.	Prisoners received from court under sentence of death and percentage change from previous year—U.S.	45
4.1.	Population-based execution rates expressed as standard scores with mean 0.0 and standard deviation 1.0, and homicide regions.	64
4.2.	Execution attributes in the context of homicide regions, expressed in two dimensions.	65
5.1.	Race adjusted execution rates per 10,000, U.S. and selected states.	73
5.2.	Execution rates as Z-scores, total population, 1876–1885.	74
5.3.	Execution rates as Z-scores, African-American population, 1876–1885.	75
5.4.	Execution rates as Z-scores, total population, 1926–1935.	76
5.5.	Execution rates as Z-scores, African-American population, 1926–1935.	77

5.6.	Distribution of African-American population, 1990, by counties.	77
5.7.	Distribution of all executions of African-Americans, by counties.	78
5.8.	Executions of women, 1632–1879.	80
5.9.	Executions of men, 1632–1879.	80
5.10.	Executions of women, 1880–1929.	81
5.11.	Executions of men, 1880–1929.	82
5.12.	Executions of women, 1930–1939.	82
5.13.	Executions of men, 1930–1939.	83
5.14.	Executions of women, 1940–1987.	83
5.15.	Executions of men, 1940–1987.	84
5.16.	Number of executions by gender, age, and period.	85
5.17.	Number of executions by gender, race, and period.	86
5.18.	Number of executions by gender and occupation.	87
5.19.	Number of executions by gender and crime.	88
5.20.	Number of executions by gender, method of execution, and period.	89
6.1.	Examples of contiguous counties.	99
7.1.	Life-without-parole and capital punishment, 1996, by states.	120
A1.	Espy File totals, 1 January 1986, by states.	128
A2.	Espy File additions, 1986–1995. Raw totals, by states.	129
A3.	Espy File additions, 1986–1995, as percentage of pre-1986 totals, by states.	130

Tables

2.1.	Highest absolute frequencies of execution by county.	23
4.1.	Contributions of two variables illustrating high (black) and low (male) chi-square values in the correspondence analysis.	67
4.2.	Total chi-square values and associated inertias.	68
5.1.	Crime weights by gender.	89
5.2.	Crime weights by period and gender.	90
5.3.	Most serious offense for which imprisoned: Whites and African-Americans, 1973–1990.	90
6.1.	Predictors of violent crime rate in 1,725 counties.	105
6.2.	Predictors of violent crime rate in 1,725 counties with capital punishment variables included.	106
6.3.	Socioeconomic and capital punishment differences as predictors of differences in violent crime rates among 293 matched county pairs.	106
7.1.	Life-without-parole (LWP) and capital punishment (CP) 1996, by states.	110

Acknowledgments

The principal source of execution data utilized here is the Espy File archived at the Inter-University Consortium for Political and Social Research (ICPSR). The data for *Executions in the United States, 1608-1987: The Espy File* were originally collected and prepared by M. Watt Espy and John Ortiz Smykla. Neither the collector of the original data nor the Consortium bear any responsibility for the analyses or interpretations presented here. Another ICPSR file was also used, and the same caveats apply: *Historical, Demographic, Economic, and Social Data: The United States, 1790-1970* [Machine-readable data file ICPSR 0003]. Data on executions since 1987 were supplied by the National Coalition to Abolish the Death Penalty, Washington D.C., and by M. Watt Espy.

The following publishers have given permission for the adaptation of their copyrighted material, as indicated: Chapter 2: Adapted in part from *Political Geography*, 14, K.D. Harries, "The last walk: A geography of execution in the United States, 1786-1985," pp. 473-495, © 1995, with kind permission from Butterworth-Heinemann Journals, Elsevier Science Ltd., The Boulevard, Langford Lane, Kidlington OX5 1GB, UK. Chapter 3: D. Cheatwood, "Capital punishment and corrections: Is there an impending crisis?" *Crime and Delinquency* 31, pp. 461-479, © 1985. Adapted by permission of Sage Publications. Chapter 4: Adapted in part from *Geoforum*, 24, K.D. Harries, "Geography, homicide, and execution: The U.S. experience," pp. 205-213, © 1993, with kind permission from Butterworth-Heinemann Journals, Elsevier Science Ltd. The Boulevard, Langford Lane, Kidlington OX5 1GB, UK. Chapter 5: Adapted in part from "Gender, execution and geography in the United States," by K.D. Harries, from *Geografiska Annaler Series B*, 74, pp. 21-29, by permission of Scandinavian University Press. Chapter 6: Adapted from D. Cheatwood, "Capital punishment and the deterrence of violence crime in comparable counties," *Criminal Justice Review*, 18, pp. 165-181, © 1993. Chapter 7: D. Cheatwood, "The life-without-parole sanction: Its current status and a research agenda." *Crime and Delinquency* 34, pp. 43-59, © 1988. Adapted by permission of Sage Publications.

1

The Issue in Context

International Perspectives

While the use of execution has declined throughout most of the First World, the United States remains an outpost—one of the last democracies—where belief in the utility of capital punishment as the ultimate deterrent is not only alive, but also practiced. The United States has, as Bohm (1991a) put it, "the dubious distinction of being the only western industrialized nation to continue to routinely sentence capital offenders to death." Although capital punishment is not used in the United States on the scale employed in, for example, Iran, China, or Nigeria (*Economist* 1989), it has experienced a resurgence in the last couple of decades while other developed nations have tended to distance themselves from the practice.

In neighboring Canada, for example, where 230 offenses had been punishable by death under British law in effect since the nineteenth century, the most recent—and last—execution was in 1962, and civilian capital punishment was abolished in 1976. In 1987, amidst calls for the reinstitution of capital punishment as a crime deterrent, the Canadian Parliament voted 148–127 not to restore the death penalty (Gendreau 1988).

In Britain, pro-capital punishment Conservative members of Parliament have been unable to forge a majority to restore the death penalty, due in part to the mellowing of older MPs and the apparent use of a pro-capital punishment position merely as a ploy to get candidates elected; once in office they tend to revert to a position opposed to hanging (*Economist* 1988). Also influential in Britain was the erroneous 1950 execution of Timothy Evans, found guilty of a murder actually committed by his neighbor, John Christie (Hook and Kahn 1989; Sorrell 1987).

The (then West) German constitution adopted in 1949 specifically excluded capital punishment. In Belgium, the last West European country retaining the death penalty in violation of the European Human Rights Convention, the government approved a draft bill to abolish it in November 1995 (Reuters 1995). Japan uses capital punishment, but sparingly, for a narrow set of crimes; typically, only two or three people are executed per year (Hook and Kahn 1989). In 1990–91, with the break-up of the Soviet Union, the death penalty was abolished in several former Soviet satellites in Eastern Europe, including Hungary and East Germany (Daly 1991). In mid-1995, Amnesty International reported that about half the countries of the world had abolished capital punishment "in law or practice." In 1994, in an estimate regarded as an underreporting, some 2,331 persons were executed in 37 countries; 1,791 were reported executed in China, 139 in Iran, and more than 100 in Nigeria; these "big three" countries accounted for 87 percent of executions worldwide (Amnesty International 1995).

In general, developed nations have come to see capital punishment as a human-rights issue, while developing countries have yet to adopt such an "advanced" position; many rulers there remain willing to use terror, including the liberal use of execution, to intimidate their opponents. Conceptually, however, this context is not directly comparable with that of the United States, in that these countries use capital punishment as a political weapon.

The United States

A complete hiatus in capital punishment occurred in the United States for nine years (1968 through 1976) around the time of the Supreme Court's 1972 *Furman v. Georgia* decision (408 U.S. 238, 1972) suspending capital punishment. Recent decades have brought its revival, with some 313 executions carried out between 1976[1] (when the death penalty was reinstated by the Supreme Court) and 1995. Between 1976 and 1983, only 11 executions occurred, but the pace then picked up markedly; the figures in all subsequent years were in double digits (U.S. Department of Justice 1991a, 10; Biskupic 1994). While the total in the period 1976–1990 (about 10 per year) represented an annual rate of execution only about one-fourth that of the preceding three-and-a-half centuries,[2] the quantity was still far from trivial. In 1990, 11 of the 36 states with capital punishment statutes executed 23 prisoners, twice the annual rate for the 1976–1990 period; by 1995 the total was up to 56. Between 1989 and 31 December, 1990, the number of prisoners under sentence of death increased 5 percent (U.S. Department of Justice 1991b). Although the trend in the number of executions has been moving erratically upward, the proportion of death row prisoners executed in any given year remains minuscule.

The Issue in Context

The 56 prisoners executed in 1995 represented less than 2 percent of the 3,000 on death row (figure 1.1).

Political Pressure

A broad renaissance of capital punishment may result from recent initiatives in the U.S. Congress and pressures on politicians to "do something" about violence, perceived by many to have reached crisis proportions. For example, a bill characterized as "anticrime" easily passed the U.S. Senate in 1991; it would have reinstated the federal death penalty, giving federal courts the power to impose it for 51 crimes, embracing 23 capital offenses that previously had been excluded owing to "procedural defects" (Dewar 1991). This action in the Senate was supported by a later House anticrime bill authorizing, like the Senate version, the death penalty for over 50 crimes. The House bill also eliminated a provision, known as the "Fairness in Death Sentencing Act," that would have allowed challenges to death sentences based on data that demonstrated the apparent existence of

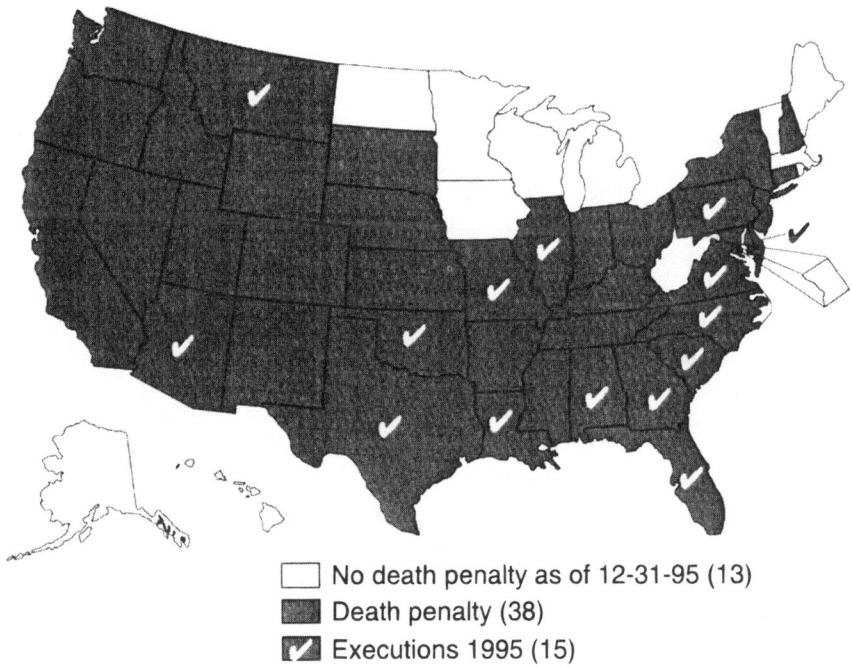

Figure 1.1. State executions and status of the death penalty in 1995.

racial discrimination in certain states. Supporters of the fairness measure pointed out that out of the 144 executions since 1976, only one was of a white for murdering an African-American (Isikoff 1991).

A *Washington Post* editorial described the House bill as "outrageous" and the Senate version as "even worse," a measure that "would throw the federal judicial system into chaos" (*Washington Post* 1991a, A26). Also in Washington, the designation of the District of Columbia as the "murder capital" of the United States led then-Mayor Sharon Pratt Dixon[3] to suggest that revival of the death penalty for drug-related homicides was an idea that "merits study" (Ragland 1991a, 1991b).[4]

Symptomatic of the fear of crime in general and of violence in particular was another round of anticrime initiatives introduced in Congress in 1994, with the most attention being given to a controversial "three strikes and you're out" provision to permanently incarcerate felons with three (federal) convictions. This legislation, as eventually enacted, increased from 2 to 60 the number of capital federal crimes; the new list included such crimes as car-jackings involving murder and drive-by shootings (Dewar 1994).

The Shelby Initiative

Personal experiences of politicians began to play into political initiatives as they or those close to them were victimized. In the most influential case, Tom Barnes, an aide to Alabama Senator Richard Shelby, was murdered in Washington D.C. in January 1992. This prompted the senator to introduce legislation providing for "tougher penalties" for murder in the District, including the restoration of execution, which had been abolished in 1962 (Shelby 1992). In late 1992, the Shelby initiative led to a referendum on capital punishment in the District of Columbia, a requirement that had been incorporated into D.C.'s appropriations bill. The bill passed by a 2-1 margin in the House of Representatives on 24 September, 1992, generating sharp opposition from political and religious leaders (Jenkins 1992a, 1992b).

As written for the 3 November, 1992, ballot, the measure was described as "one of the broadest in the country" and included juveniles. In its breadth, it contained many more criteria of eligibility compared to capital statutes elsewhere; essentially any person convicted of first-degree homicide would be eligible (Harriston 1992). Although thousands of African-American males, most young, had been homicide victims in the District of Columbia in recent years, it was the death of one politically connected white man—the senator's aide—that led to an attempt to change the law. Ultimately, Washington D.C. voters easily rejected the measure at the November 1992 general election.

The political turn to the right embodied in the Republican *Contract with America*, a key plank in the November 1994 Congressional election, presaged a hardening of attitudes toward the death penalty likely to find expression both through more executions in states with capital punishment and more states adopting the death penalty.[5] Public sentiment increasingly leans toward shortening the protracted appeals process, and a small amount of anecdotal evidence even identified sentiment in favor of executing children as an example to their peers (British Broadcasting Corporation Overseas Service, 1995).

Contradictions

Texas, having emerged as the top-ranking execution state, exemplifies some of the contradictions surrounding the issue. The execution of Jesse Jacobs on 4 January 1995 was remarkable because the prosecution acknowledged that he did not commit the murder for which he was convicted and also because the State of Texas had at one time or another supported two different versions of the crime scenario (Pressley 1995). Jacobs and his sister participated in the abduction and murder of Etta Ann Urdiales in May 1987. While it was determined that Jacobs's sister pulled the trigger, and both were convicted, he was executed, while she was found guilty of involuntary manslaughter (Amnesty International 1996). U.S. Supreme Court Justice Stevens, dissenting from the majority that declined to hear the appeal, noted that: "It would be fundamentally unfair to execute a person on the basis of a factual determination that the state has formally disavowed. I find this course of events deeply troubling" (Spectacle 1996).

In similar vein, a *Washington Post* editorial noted:

> As the new Congress rushes to speed executions and emasculate habeas corpus, this case is, unfortunately for the defendant, a terrible example of what can go wrong when the zeal for punishment outweighs the glaring evidence that there has been a grievous miscarriage of justice. (*Washington Post* 1995)

Yet even within the United States is evidence of a certain residual political ambivalence, given the dichotomy between the 38 states with capital punishment statutes on the books and the 13 (including Washington D.C.) without (fig. 1.1 and appendix 3). Underlying the pace of executions is the concept that "social and political cultures" of the states are just as significant as legal traditions and precedents in the role of determinants. The long appeals process and the actual low rate of executions exemplifies ambivalence on the part of both the legal establishment and the public with respect to the issue (Kamen 1989).

Backlog

As Keve (1992) has noted, the low rate of executions leads to a mounting backlog on death rows which testifies to our collective unwillingness to put into effect the bloodbath necessary to make a small and stable death row population that would evolve if the capital punishment system were working smoothly. Keve pointed out that of the 38 (as of 1991) of the possible 53 (50 states, plus D.C., the federal courts, and the military) jurisdictions with the death penalty, 36 had collectively 2,547 prisoners on death rows. If 25 per year were executed, 102 years would be needed to eliminate the backlog without any net additions, a situation characterized as a pretense: "In effect we are resorting to an occasional execution to keep ourselves persuaded that we are being tough on crime." When Thorsten Sellin made a similar comparison in 1965, he wrote that "it would take nearly 48 years to expedite the executions at the present rate, not counting the annual contingents of new admissions during the period" (Sellin 1967, 239). The pipeline seems to be clogging. (See chapter 3 for an in-depth analysis of this issue.)

Cost

Keve (1992) also underscored the economic aspects of the death penalty in his description of the widely misunderstood or simply unknown fact that capital punishment is more expensive than imprisonment. New York capital cases are estimated to cost nearly $2 million even without complete appellate review. A similar cost has been reported for Texas, and it has been estimated that the death penalty process costs California about $90 million per year (Von Drehle 1995a; see also Verhovek 1995). Florida calculated that each execution there costs some $3.18 million. If incarceration is estimated to cost $17,000/year (a figure that Keve disputes because of the fixed nature of most prison costs), a comparable statistic for life imprisonment of 40 years would be $680,000. Although details vary from state to state, we can conclude with confidence that both incarceration and execution are very expensive and that execution is not the quick fix to reduce costs of dealing with criminals that many might hope or expect.

Although most rhetoric in recent years has come from death penalty proponents, retired Supreme Court Justice Harry Blackmun stirred controversy in 1994 with his highly publicized declaration of his position in opposition to execution, a position atypical of those in high public office, and, a cynic might note, not a position Justice Blackmun could have taken while an active justice (Biskupic 1994; see also Will 1994, in response to Blackmun).

Opinion Polls

Opinion poll data offer another indicator of changes in the public attitude toward capital punishment. In a detailed analysis of Gallup polls conducted between 1936 and 1986, Bohm (1991b, 135) noted that race, socioeconomic status, gender, politics, and region showed the greatest differences over the 50-year period: ". . . whites, wealthier people, males, Republicans, and Westerners have tended to support the death penalty more than blacks, poorer people, females, Democrats, and Southerners."

Very recent data confirmed these findings although regional differences appear to have diminished somewhat; 1995 Gallup data showed a spread of only 3 percentage points among the four regions: East, Midwest, South, and West (Maguire and Pastore 1995).

Death Penalty Approval Up

A longitudinal comparison of Gallup polls taken at intervals over the period of 1936 through 1988 showed that the proportion favoring the death penalty declined between 1936 and 1966 from about 60–65 percent to about 40 percent. The years after 1966 showed a fairly steady rise to about 80 percent approval by 1988. These data are partially illustrated in figure 1.2, showing "attitudes toward the death penalty for persons convicted of murder" for certain years between 1953 and 1995. After a high approval level in 1953 (68 percent), approval ratings fell off somewhat in 1956 and then began trending erratically upward to around the 80 percent level in 1994–95. Disapproval ratings mirrored this trend (Gallup poll data from Maguire and Pastore 1995, table 2.56).

If college freshmen are a bellwether group in terms of opinions that might be expected in future polls that will include older age cohorts, then figure 1.3 is informative. Two observations can be made. First, female freshmen are steadily less supportive of capital punishment than are their male cohorts, although the difference has narrowed in recent years. This is consistent with the Gallup poll data cited above. Second, support of capital punishment increased dramatically following the *Furman* hiatus in the 1970s. We might speculate that, during those years, the students then in middle and high school were influenced by parental displeasure at the suspension of capital punishment,

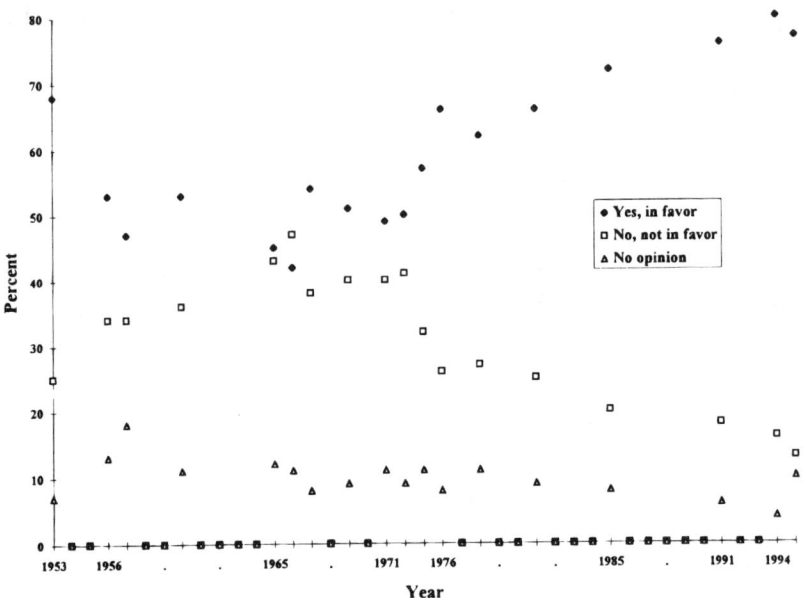

Figure 1.2. Attitudes toward the death penalty for persons convicted of murder. *Data source*: Maguire and Pastore, 1995, Table 2.56. Gallup poll data; some years are missing.

and people were therefore able to "get away with murder." Perhaps they then carried this opinion forward into the 1978 poll. (See also Sanchez 1995.)

Other poll data suggest that support for the death penalty among police chiefs and county sheriffs is rather lukewarm, with only 34 percent agreeing with the statement: "I support the death penalty and think it works well." Some 58 percent agreed with the statement: "Philosophically, I support the death penalty, but I don't think it is an effective law enforcement tool in practice" (Maguire and Pastore 1995, table 2.61).

Roper poll data for 1989 and 1990, like the Gallup polls, similarly indicated high approval ratings (74 percent) for both years (Maguire and Flanagan 1991, 199–201). Ellsworth and Gross (1994) confirmed these trends and also noted that public opinion has become more favorable toward the execution of both youths and the mentally retarded. Furthermore, support for the death penalty has tended to parallel increases in violent crime. By and large, they note, "Most people care a great deal about the death penalty but know little about it, and have no particular desire to know" (p. 40).

The Issue in Context

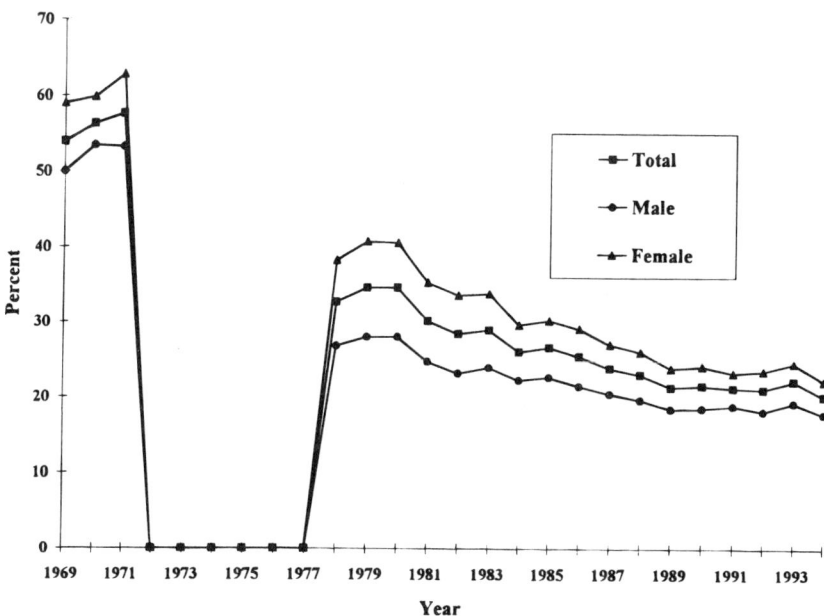

Figure 1.3. Percent of college freshmen reporting that capital punishment should be abolished 1969–94. *Data source*: Maguire and Pastore 1995, table 2.103. No data for 1972–77. Based on annual data from Day, Astin, and Korn.

Newsweek opinion poll data on capital punishment in 1995 indicated sharp qualitative differences in responses depending on the circumstances relating to cases. Sixty-three percent favored the death penalty for Susan Smith, convicted of drowning of her two children in John D. Long Lake in Union, South Carolina. Seventy-nine percent favored death for Timothy McVeigh, if convicted in the Oklahoma City Federal Building bombing case. However, when respondents were asked to take into account hypothetical circumstances involving the convicted person, such as their abuse as a child, emotional imbalance, or insanity, approval dropped to the 46–48 percent range (Morganthau *et al.* 1995).

Similarly, Sandys and McGarrell (1995) found in a survey of 514 Indiana citizens that, although "general favorability" toward capital punishment was some 76 percent, only 9 percent of capital punishment proponents were firmly committed under all circumstances. For example, 74 percent of those surveyed agreed "at least somewhat" with the proposition that "the death penalty should not be imposed on a mentally retarded person," and 51 percent agreed that juveniles (under 18) should not be sentenced to death. Support for capital punishment also softened when alternatives, such as life without parole (see chapter 7) were presented.

In general, changes in public approval of capital punishment have correlated quite closely with changes in the national homicide rate, which declined from the mid-1930s to the mid-1960s and then rose sharply until about 1980 (U.S. Department of Justice 1988; see also figure 2.10). This relationship encourages the conclusion that public approval of capital punishment is to some extent an understandable reaction to fear of violent crime.

Given the high level of approval of capital punishment by the public at large and their political representatives and the disparity between the United States and other developed countries on this question, a geographic perspective of the issue is illuminating. This viewpoint conveys a sense of the extraordinary degree of place-to-place variation in execution, a problem that continues to be an intensely controversial topic in the policy arena. Ultimately, this place-to-place variation is the expression of not only interstate differences in laws, but also interstate (and intrastate) applications of those laws, themes that are developed throughout this book. Such variations imply abrogation of the constitutional right of equal protection under the law, notwithstanding the often-heard view to the effect that people who commit capital offenses are "taking their chances."

Capital Punishment as a Moral Decision

The basic decision about the existence and use of capital punishment is inescapably a moral one. There are questions about capital punishment that can be answered empirically; whether it does or does not deter crime or brutalize society, whether it is justly and responsibly administered, and whether it can incapacitate without error. This book addresses some of these empirical questions whose answers may help an individual or a society make more informed decisions about whether they are "for" or "against" capital punishment.

But no data, whatever the quantity, can resolve or abrogate the fundamental moral choice that must be made regarding the use of capital punishment. Whatever conclusions we reach about the function, dysfunction, administration, or uneven distribution of capital punishment, these conclusions never answer the question of whether we should execute.

Our goal is to offer empirical material that relates to the use of capital punishment in the United States in the hope that the data will allow for more reasoned conclusions. Our focus is on the central fact that capital punishment is differentially distributed through the

The Issue in Context 11

states and counties of the United States, and this distribution reflects different cultures of both politics and violence. What these differences mean in practice is that the probability of a murderer or other capital offender being executed is zero in some places and better than zero in others.

Theory/Deterrence

The main theory supporting capital punishment is *deterrence*, the idea that potential killers will fail to become actual killers because of the fear of one dire consequence. This is a much-visited topic. Notable treatments have included the book-length debate between Ernest van den Haag and John Conrad (van den Haag and Conrad 1983) which arrived at no definitive answer with respect to the deterrence issue. For example, Conrad wrote: "Conceding as he does that statistical proof of the deterrent effect of the death penalty is wanting, Professor van den Haag asks us to rely on common sense . . ." (p. 71). Van den Haag, for his part, was convinced that "harsher penalties are more deterrent than milder ones" (p. 299).

A Question of Values

Zimring and Hawkins (1986) noted that, ultimately, the death penalty is justified not on the grounds of its deterrent effect, but on the basis of social values relating to morality and justice. They reviewed Sellin's (1967) approach to the analysis of deterrence through comparisons of homicide rates in states with and without capital punishment, and Isaac Erlich's regression analysis in response and his conclusion that some eight victims would have been saved by the deterrent effect of each capital punishment in the period 1933–67 (Erlich 1975). On the basis of their extensive review, Zimring and Hawkins concluded that:

> The presence or absence of the capital threat and the low levels of execution accompanying that threat have not produced any significant variation in homicide rates. . . . There is room for debate only about whether the marginal deterrent effect is nil, or very small in relation to total homicide volume . . . the effect cannot be major. (pp. 180–181)

More recent analysis has reinforced the position that the capital punishment process does not deter capital crimes. Bailey and Peterson (1994) and Haney and Logan (1994) have brought the social science evidence together in a convincing rejection of the deterrence hypothesis. (See also Hook and Kahn 1989, chapter 5 pp. 41–53.) We hope to shed additional light on the deterrence issue by combining temporal and spatial perspectives, each of which illuminates the issue differently.

Although the question will be examined in more detail later, it should be noted that comparisons between trends in homicide rates and execution rates (in order to draw conclusions about an assumed relationship) are fraught with difficulty due to the influence of hidden variables. For example, homicide may increase as a response to

- an increase in the supply of young, poor males in the population—a demographic phenomenon;
- changes in the culture of drugs or alcohol, most recently demonstrated by the crack cocaine epidemic that started about 1988 in major American cities;
- "improved" firearm technology: more (and more lethal) bullets capable of being shot at targets more rapidly than ever before, making mortality more likely.[6]

Furthermore, any society will have a "background," or minimum, level of homicide, below which homicide rates are unlikely to go under any circumstances. Empirical evidence based on world homicide rates suggests that this background rate may be about 1 or 2 per 100,000. These are the events that are most likely tied to interpersonal conflicts among family members or between paramours. Such events are generally crimes of passion, committed on the spur of the moment and presumably unlikely to be deterred by a cool analysis of consequences. When secular conditions such as the state of the economy and unemployment levels are taken into account, trends in homicide or other violent crimes are seen to be complex indeed, defying any simplistic trend comparison.

Capital Punishment and Geography

Why a geography of capital punishment? The most clear-cut response is that capital punishment has a distinctive geography, ranging along a continuum from abolitionist to relatively frequent executions, and it is clear that the various elements of American culture that have an impact on capital punishment exhibit frequently sharp spatial variation, particularly in terms of state laws. These variations can show up in more subtle ways, too, having to do with customary interracial relationships, for example, or the moral, religious, and political philosophy of the state's founders and the imprimatur, or otherwise, that they put on capital punishment.

When it comes to making changes in capital statutes, some states are leaders, others laggards, providing a kind of spatio-temporal arbitrariness to the evolution of capital punishment. For example, when the U.S. Supreme Court rendered its 1972 decision in *Furman v. Georgia*, striking down capital statutes in some 40 jurisdictions, it handed down the Court's longest decision. "Rambling and inchoate," according to Von Drehle (1995b), it was not, perhaps, surprising (given the historically high rate of executions in the South) that it was a Southern state, Florida, that rushed to reinstate the death penalty in a way that would withstand Supreme Court scrutiny. A Florida legislative commission adopted the concepts of "aggravating" and "mitigating" circumstances to be weighed in making death penalty decisions in response to what were perceived to be criteria implied in *Furman's* 50,000 words. As the first legislation passed in response to *Furman*, the Florida law became a model, and "immediately, officials from across the country began calling Florida for advice and guidance" (Von Drehle 1995b, 13). Thus, Florida was the innovator, triggering diffusion of its new law to other jurisdictions.

A geographic perspective is important because of the place-specific cultural rootedness of the death penalty described above. Capital punishment in the United States today is not an abstract imperial dogma handed down from on high, but rather a hodgepodge of state laws written or plagiarized in response to *Furman* and mediated by local or regional political, religious, and moral philosophies expressed through raw political pressure. These laws contain different provisions for aggravating and mitigating circumstances and allow the death penalty for different sets of offenses. The laws vary in their complexity and therefore in their susceptibility to technical challenges. As the case studies of Virginia, Maryland, and Washington, D.C. illustrate later in this book (chapter 2, pp. 34–37), geographic gradients in the laws of capital punishment are, to say the least, remarkable, in that identical behaviors may (Virginia, Maryland) or will not (Washington, D.C.) result in execution, depending on which side of a political boundary the behavior occurred.

It is not unreasonable to believe that many persons subject to capital trials were not even aware at the time of their offense whether they were in a jurisdiction with capital punishment. After all, many political boundaries, such as that between Washington, D.C. and Maryland, are quite unclear in the minds of residents. For example, who would know, without research, that the boundary between Maryland and Virginia is the right bank of the Potomac River with the result that all the river, where Maryland abuts Virginia, is in Maryland? Thus, Maryland has jurisdiction over any crime taking place in or on the river or its bridges. Such esoterica may seem irrelevant, but they are actually quite germane when decisions must be made about who will charge a suspect and what the consequences of conviction may be. The boundary issue also begs the question of how often offenders have any sense of how important the location of the crime may be in terms of its legal consequences. Such awareness could mean the difference between life and death for the offender for an act committed along, for example, the boundaries of either Maryland or Virginia with Washington, D.C., which lacks the death penalty.

Directions

We incorporate both geographic and historical perspectives on capital punishment under the assumption that opinion and policy are best informed by understanding both *where* things happened and *when* they happened, in addition to developing some sense of *why*. We can visualize two continua in terms of attitudes toward capital punishment, one in space, the other in time. Attitudes will vary among places or communities, and over time. Thus, in the course of time, a particular community may experience shifts in attitudes from pro to con and back again as political tides and demographic changes exert their influence. While there is no shortage of historical treatments of capital punishment, what is missing is a treatment that puts both space and time together. This is an important juxtaposition, we would argue, in that the expression of culture is specific to both; neither aggregated historical trends nor the experiences of specific communities should be looked at in isolation.

This book attempts to examine the death penalty question through these dual filters of space and time in an effort to capture and interpret change and provide some of the foundation needed for review of public policy. Underlying this posture is the naive assumption that public policy is informed by social scientific analysis; the reality is that some policy is so informed, and some is not. Capital punishment is an issue influenced more than most by emotional public responses and political pandering to those responses, with candidates for office seemingly competing with each other in terms of who can promise the most severe punishments for criminals, a natural outcome of an era in which crime is an unusually powerful issue.

Our approach is heavily empirical, with some of the data we use drawn from the archives of the Inter-University Consortium for Political and Social Research (ICPSR) at the University of Michigan. Of these resources, the Espy file, compiled by Watt Espy in Headland, Alabama, is the foremost (Espy and Smykla 1987). This file is the product of a remarkable effort to document all the executions in American history, initially covering 14,570 executions in the period from 1608 to

1987. None of the data sources is perfect, and, as is typical of social science data, there are omissions, the most common of which is omission through undercounting, whether in census resources or in the Espy file.[7]

In addition to our emphasis on the integration of geographic and historical perspectives, we also stress the visualization of data and analysis relating to capital punishment. Indeed, we could scarcely do justice to the geographic viewpoint without translating information into maps, just as the temporal dimension is often best presented with the aid of various time-based charts. The combination of an integrated spatio-temporal view and emphasis on visualization gives this analysis a fresh approach and one that we hope will have some small effect in influencing policy.

In case it is not obvious already, our research and reading have led us toward an anti-death penalty position. While we agree that in the social sciences it is virtually impossible to "prove" anything, the weight of evidence accumulated long before we put pen to paper suggested that capital punishment could not be clearly shown to deter violence, the attribute most hoped for by the public and one that we assume to be its strongest selling point, along with revenge and elimination or its euphemistic synonym, incapacitation. The latter motives are jaded in their practice by errors in the identification of the guilty and the actual execution of innocents. (On this point, see Radelet, Bedau, and Putnam 1994.)

The presence of error and high dollar costs tends to make capital punishment both morally and economically indefensible. We also subscribe to the notion that no science, and perhaps least of all social science, is value-free, so it is imperative that we make our position clear at the outset to enable readers to take our beliefs and preconceptions into account. This having been said, we present our analysis in what we believe to be a straightforward way with no attempt to select only information that would bolster the "anti" cause.

Notes

1. The first actual execution was in 1977.
2. 14,570 executions/379 years equals 38.4 per year. Given that the base population is now relatively large, the population-adjusted rate is very small compared to previous centuries.
3. Mayor Dixon later married and adopted her husband's surname: Kelly.
4. No execution had occurred in Washington, D.C. since 1957 (Harriston 1992).
5. Presidential candidates Bush and Clinton both supported capital punishment in their 1992 campaigns. As General Colin Powell flirted with possible presidential candidacy in the fall of 1995, he answered immediately and affir-

matively an interviewer's question asking whether he favored capital punishment. Senator Robert Dole, de facto republican presidential nominee in early 1996, made a campaign stop at the death row at San Quentin prison in California in order to urge swifter justice for those sentenced to death.

6. The development of trauma centers has tended to offset the influence of greater fire power but to what extent is unknown.

7. In a personal communication (26 June, 1995), M. Watt Espy noted that the Inter-university Consortium for Political and Social Research (ICPSR) at the University of Michigan had included what he described as inaccurate and incomplete data as "the Espy File." Maps reflecting the new cases discovered by Mr. Espy since the release of the ICPSR file are shown in Appendix I.

2

The Historical Geography of Capital Punishment in America

This chapter examines four broad issues. The *first* is a review of the attributes of persons executed and the historical geography of capital punishment, by eras, from the late eighteenth century until the mid-1980s. The *second* is an assessment of recent trends in the geography of capital punishment. The *third* is the issue of the relationship between *rates* of homicide and *rates* of execution, which permits some consideration of the deterrent effect, if any, of capital punishment.[1] *Finally*, we consider interstate variation in the context of a case study of the Maryland-Washington, D.C.-Virginia region.

Data Sources and Method

Executions

This research was made possible by the availability of a comprehensive data base—known as the Espy File—of executions in the United States from the 1608 shooting in Jamestown of the mutinous Captain George Kendall to mid-1987. M. Watt Espy, beginning work at his home in Headland, Alabama, in 1970, compiled by hand the most complete file on executions known to date. Data were gathered from state departments of corrections, newspapers, microfilmed records, county histories, and various other archives. However, it is recognized that the record is incomplete; Espy did not discover some executions from the earlier part of the time frame, and he confirmed some executions with incomplete data. Even some relatively recent executions, such as those carried out with portable electric chairs in Louisiana and Mississippi in the 1940s and 1950s, may not be accurately accounted for. The data file was ultimately transferred to the University of Alabama Law Center in 1977 for computerization, updating, and distribution through the Inter-University Consortium for Political and Social Research (ICPSR) at the University of Michigan (Espy and Smykla 1987). The complete file recorded 14,570 executions, of which 13,329 are included in the analytical part of this paper, which intentionally and necessarily excludes the first 178 years of the record because census data (used for rate calculations) were not available until 1790.[2]

Census Data

Data from the Espy File are interfaced with census data drawn from another ICPSR resource: *Historical, Demographic, Economic, and Social Data: The United States, 1790 to 1970*, in combination with data from the 1980 Census of Population (U.S. Bureau of the Census 1984). Homicide rates employed in part of the analysis were drawn from *Vital Statistics of the United States* (Rand 1992).

The decennial censuses of population that began in 1790 provided the basis for the calculation of rates of execution specific to the population for the nation as a whole and for its component states. For the purpose of this analysis, a decade of execution data was attached to each census; thus, executions for the years from 1786 through 1795 were aggregated and assigned to the 1790 Census; for the 1800 Census, executions for 1796 through 1805 were accumulated, and so on. Thus, each of 20 censuses, 1790 through 1980, became an approximate temporal midpoint for the clustering of execution data and the calculation of population-specific rates. Hence, the study period spans the earliest and latest bounds of these data aggregation decades: 1786 and 1985. The data thus derived were then used to assemble charts and the maps forming the raw materials for the interpretations that follow.

An Overview of Execution

Basic Attributes of Persons Executed

Several characteristics of the 13,329 subjects of this analysis demand comment. First, the population was overwhelmingly male (97.4 percent) with a modal age cohort of 20–29, from which some 23 percent of all offenders were drawn, followed by the 30–39 age group (12.7 percent). However, the age of almost 51 percent of those enumerated was unknown with sufficient precision to be included in the record. African-Americans were heavily overrepresented with respect to their proportion of the population, constituting nearly half, with whites making up 40 percent and other races 10 percent. The occupational structure of those for whom occupation could be determined (and over 52 percent could not be) was heavily biased toward lower status employment. Indeed, convicted offenders, or those with the status of convict, escaped convict, ex-convict, or parolee, accounted for 5.3 percent of those executed. However, slaves made up nearly 10 percent and were the largest single "occupation" group.

Of the 39 specific crimes for which executions have occurred since 1608, by far the most prevalent are murder, accounting for over 60 percent, and robbery-murder (18.2 percent). If burglary-murder and rape-murder are included to create a generic murder classification, that grouping accounts for 82.3 percent of documented executions.

National Patterns

According to Schneider and Smykla (1991), the profile of the raw frequency of executions presented by the Espy File may be divided into four eras: *Growth* (to 1879), *Stability* (1880–1929), *Peak* (1930–1939), and *Decline* (since 1940). During the growth period, the general trend was upward, although considerable fluctuation is evident (figure 2.1). The period of stability was also marked by major variation, but the overall trend was not one of marked increase. However, new maxima were reached, notably in 1902 (147 executions) and 1905 (156). In the

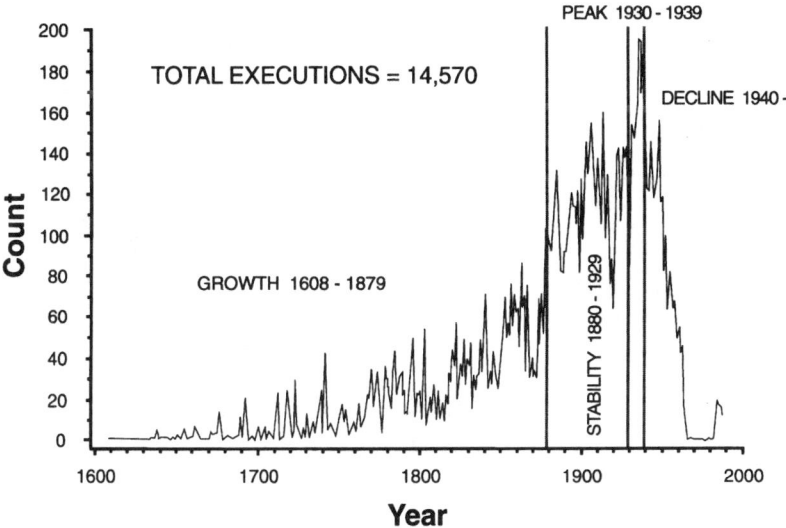

Figure 2.1. Annual execution frequencies, United States, 1608–1985. *Data source*: Espy and Smykla 1987.

peak period, executions reached their all-time high in the United States in 1935–36, with 197 and 196 incidents, respectively. Executions remained quite frequent, with over 100 in each year except 1950 (83) until 1951; after that year, the total never again approached 100. In terms of regional distribution, the South census region has had the most executions in all decades since 1800 (Schneider and Smykla 1991, 9), a pattern broadly coincidental with the geography of murder (Harries 1988; 1992a).

County Geography

The geography of execution is represented cartographically in a set of four maps depicting execution frequencies by county, by era (figures 2.2–2.5). Each choropleth map has three levels of shading representing, for each era: 1) levels of execution above the mean of all counties with executions; 2) other counties with executions (at or below the mean), and 3) counties without executions. The growth era (figure 2.2) encompasses a period of 271 years that includes the colonial period and the first 103 years of the republic. Hence, the pattern shows particularly heavy concentrations in the colonial region, with Pennsylvania and

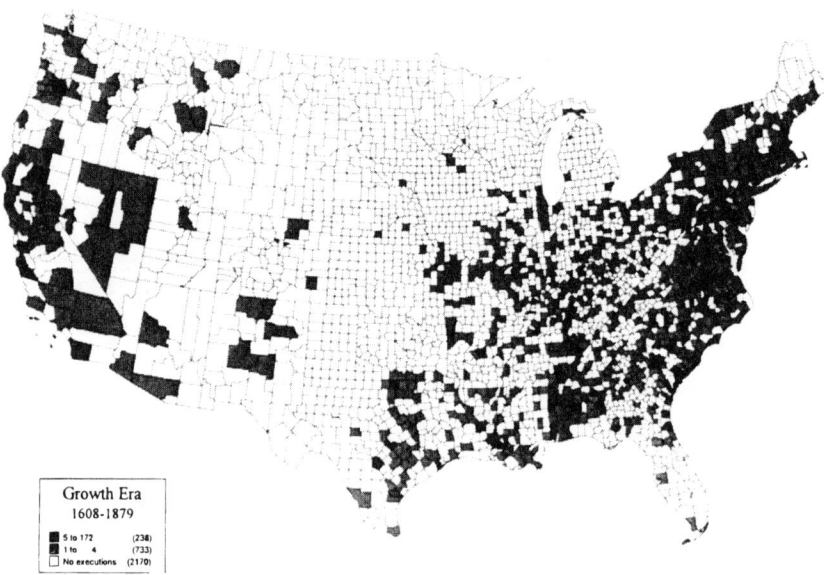

Figure 2.2. Execution frequencies by U.S. counties, Growth Era (to 1879). *Data source for figures 2.2–2.5*: Espy and Smykla 1987.

Historical Geography of Capital Punishment

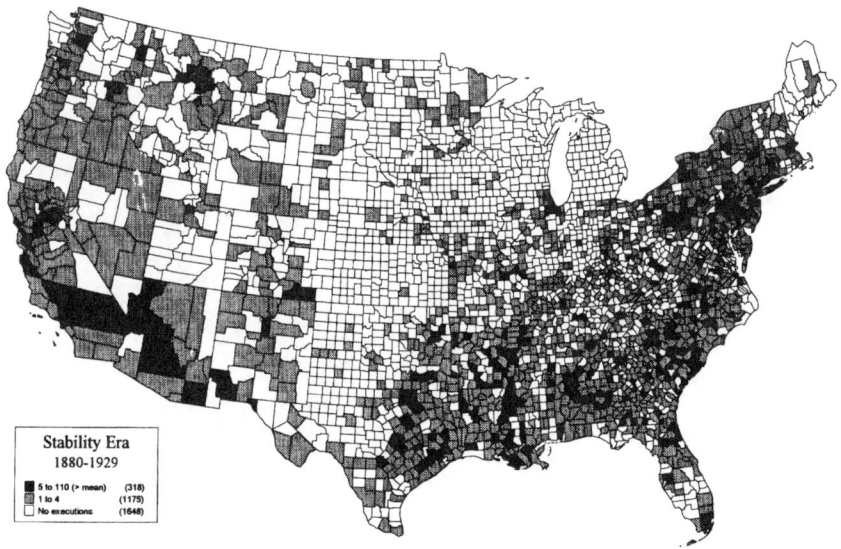

Figure 2.3. Execution frequencies by U.S. counties, Stability Era, 1880–1929.

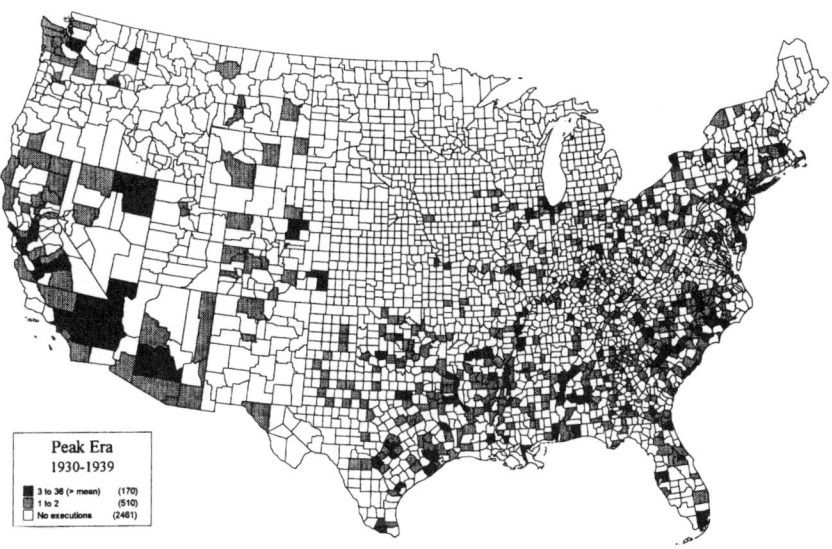

Figure 2.4. Execution frequencies by U.S. counties, Peak Era, 1930s.

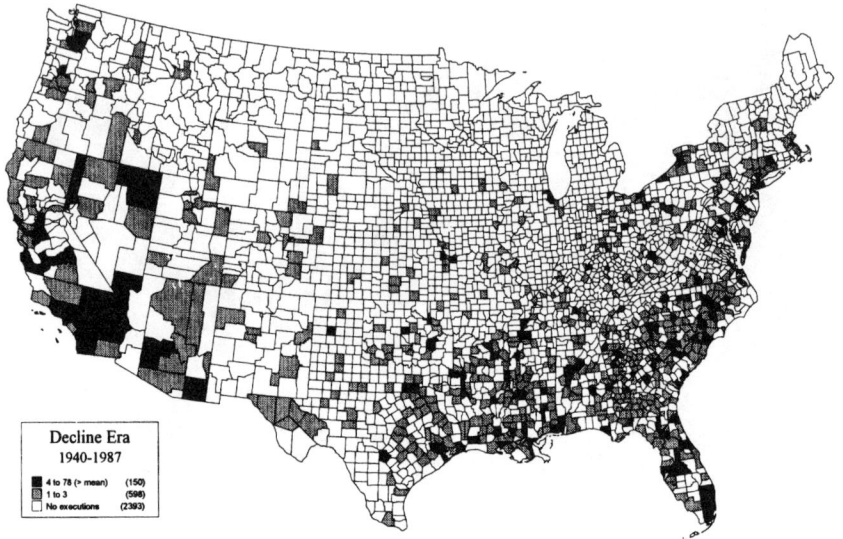

Figure 2.5. Execution frequencies by U.S. counties, Decline Era (since 1940).

Virginia notable for the extent of contiguous counties above the mean for the era.

The half-century constituting the stability era (1880–1929) is characterized by the most extensive geographic coverage of the four eras. In relation to the earlier era, settlement and accompanying governmental institutions were more extensive and fully developed. For example, Oklahoma did not become a state until 1907 and therefore first shows evidence of capital punishment in the stability era map (figure 2.3). Also, during this era capital punishment was widely accepted and not subject to the legal challenges that would come later.

The peak era (1930–39) suggests a heavily southern emphasis in relation to both counties with executions and those counties above the mean for counties with executions in the period (figure 2.4).[3] The decline era map (figure 2.5) is similar, but suggests an even stronger southern bias, with extensive blocks of contiguous execution counties in the Carolinas, Florida, Georgia, Alabama, Louisiana, Mississippi, and Texas. Thus, some evidence suggests that the South has emerged in the twentieth century as an execution region, mirroring its demonstrated prominence as a high homicide area. Historically, a crude dichotomy emerges, with execution convictions concentrated in large cities on one hand and relatively anomalous, predominantly southern, smaller population centers on the other.

Nine of the 17 counties with at least 75 executions overall were in the South (table 2.1).

Bohm (1991b, 136) has noted that "variations in aggregate death penalty opinions over time are best explained by social events." If opinion is indeed thus influenced, one may look to social events, or social events in concert with dominant contemporary ideologies, to assist in developing an understanding of trends in capital punishment. The period between the Revolution and the Civil War, for example, coinciding roughly with the growth era, was characterized by constant conflict over capital punishment. Beccaria's *An Essay on Crimes and*

Table 2.1. Highest absolute frequencies of execution by county.

State	County	Frequency
New York	New York	393
Pennsylvania	Philadelphia	246
Illinois	Cook	173
Massachusetts	Suffolk	167
South Carolina	Charleston	167
Louisiana	Orleans	153
New York	Kings	123
Washington D.C.	Washington D.C.	118
Georgia	Fulton	117
California	Los Angeles	116
Pennsylvania	Allegheny	101
Alabama	Jefferson	100
Arkansas	Sebastian	94
California	San Francisco	86
Texas	Harris	84
Maryland	Baltimore City	78
Kentucky	Jefferson	75

Data source: Espy and Smykla 1987.

Punishments (1801) was influential, advocating the role of deterrence but also arguing that the death penalty was ineffectual. Initially accepted, advocates of the death penalty were by 1820 disillusioned with it and sought alternative rationales for capital punishment. A parallel development of style, if not substance, was the private conduct of executions in the 1830s, interpreted as a reflection of the sensibilities of the middle class (Masur 1989). Events such as the assassinations of Lincoln and Garfield or, in the twentieth century, Huey Long and John and Robert Kennedy could be seen as provoking a public demand for tougher responses, including capital punishment. However, attempting to link upticks in execution to single events is generally an exercise in futility, compounded by possible confusion over whether executions are represented by raw frequencies or population-adjusted rates. (See under *Homicide and Execution*, below, for further discussion of this point.)

Why did executions manifest their numerical (if not rate) peak in the 1930s? Drawing connections to the Great Depression is unavoidable. With 16 percent of the labor force unemployed in 1931, and sharp declines in marriage, birth, and divorce rates, the 1930s were a decade of social turmoil, engendered by the New Deal, numerous strikes and, in Europe, the shadow of fascism. It was "a major crisis of the capitalist system" (Simon 1967), and the wave of executions in the decade could be seen as the "control" response of the establishment. The novelist John Dos Passos (cited in Simon 1967, 88) implied this connection in *The Big Money* (published in 1936) when he wrote "they have built the electricchair [sic] and hired the executioner to throw the switch." It should also be noted that Prohibition (1920–33) overlapped with the depression period, and an increase in capital punishment could be interpreted in part as a response to the gang violence associated with illicit alcohol trafficking. Interpretation of the recent history of capital punishment is less speculative, with landmark events such as *Furman v. Georgia* followed by the reformulation of capital statutes and the gradual escalation of executions as an inevitable consequence when seen in the context of increased violence—in particular, increased stranger-to-stranger violence.

Methods of Execution: Origin and Diffusion

Electrocution

Prior to 1900, hanging was the most common mode of execution, but technological innovation, including the central generation of electricity, made possible the invention of the electric chair. The first execution in the electric chair (1890) resulted from a conviction in Erie County, New York, following the 1888 approval of the method and the abolition of hanging by the New York legislature. The electric chair was introduced in the name of humaneness and practicality (Paternoster 1991). Subsequent electrocution-related convictions then took place in New York City (1891), and Monroe, Orange, Warren, and Kings Counties, New York (1892). Seven electrocutions followed in New York state in 1893; in all, 29 electrocutions occurred in New York state between 1890 and 1897 before the practice was adopted in Ohio (figure 2.6). Electrocution was adopted mainly in the East and South, and by 1930 more than half the states with capital punishment were using it (Paternoster 1991; figure 2.6).

The "humaneness" of the electric chair has always been open to some question. To cite but one (recent) example, on 23 August, 1991, Virginia's 83-year-old electric chair was used to execute Derick Lynn Peterson, sentenced to die for a supermarket robbery-murder in 1982. Peterson was given 1,725 volts, then a separate, longer shock of 240 volts. Following this, the prison doctor still found a pulse, and another pair of shocks had to be administered (*Washington Post* 1991b).

Gas Chamber

The use of lethal gas originated in Nevada with a law passed in 1921; the first execution using this method took place in 1924 (figure 2.7), based on a conviction in Mineral County. The pattern of diffusion is rather odd, with most adoptions in the West, where electrocution had *not* been adopted. Arizona (first execution by the new method, 1934) and Colorado (also 1934) followed Nevada, but adoption then jumped to the east coast, where North Carolina became an isolated adopter in 1936, surrounded by electrocution states (cf. figure 2.6). Then, Wyoming, Missouri, Oregon, and California followed between 1937 and 1939. (See also Bowers 1974.)

Lethal Injection

Like the introduction of electrocution and lethal gas before it, lethal injection was also viewed as a more efficient and humane way of dispatching the convicted. Oklahoma was the first state to adopt lethal injection (1977), followed by Texas, where the first such execution was in 1982 (Paternoster 1991). Today, lethal injection is the dominant method, now approved for use in 28 states, including New York, where capital punishment was recently reinstated.

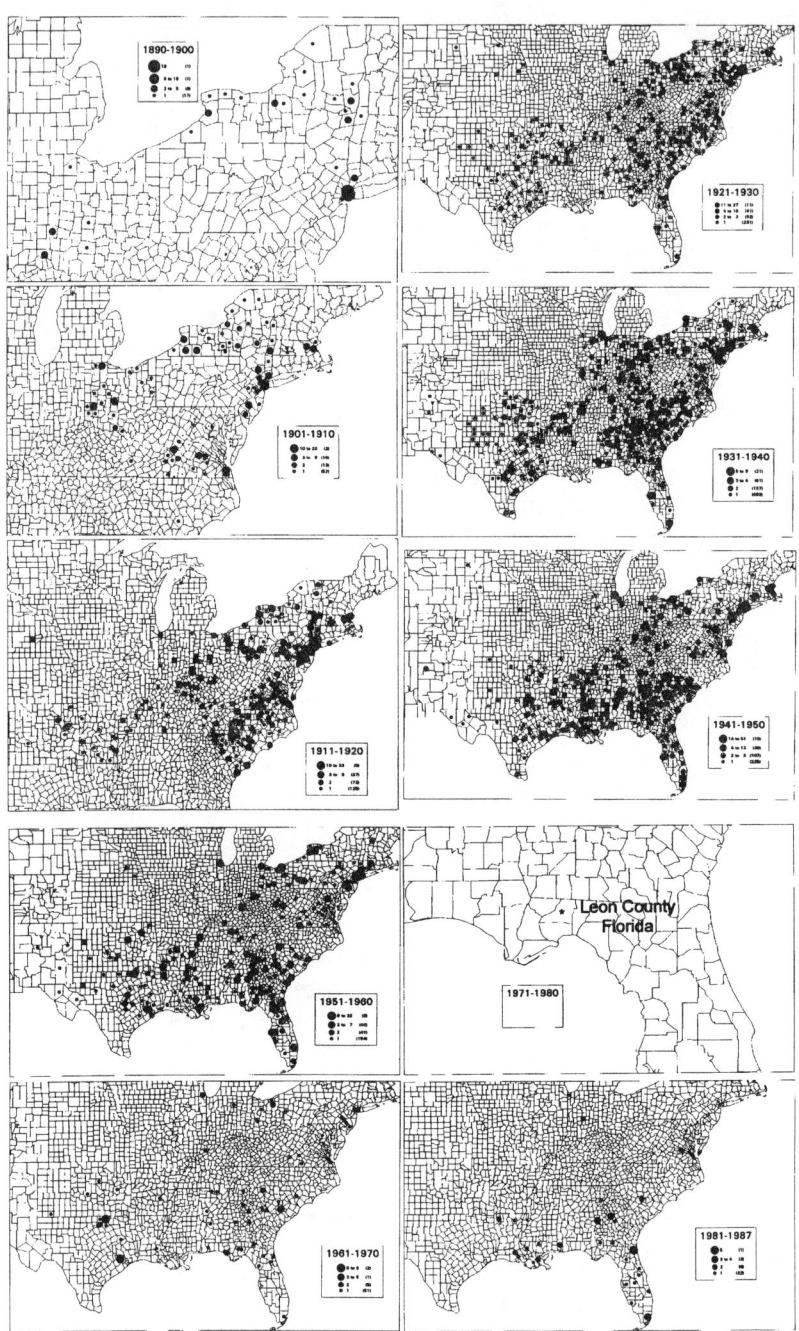

Figure 2.6. Origin and diffusion of electrocution.

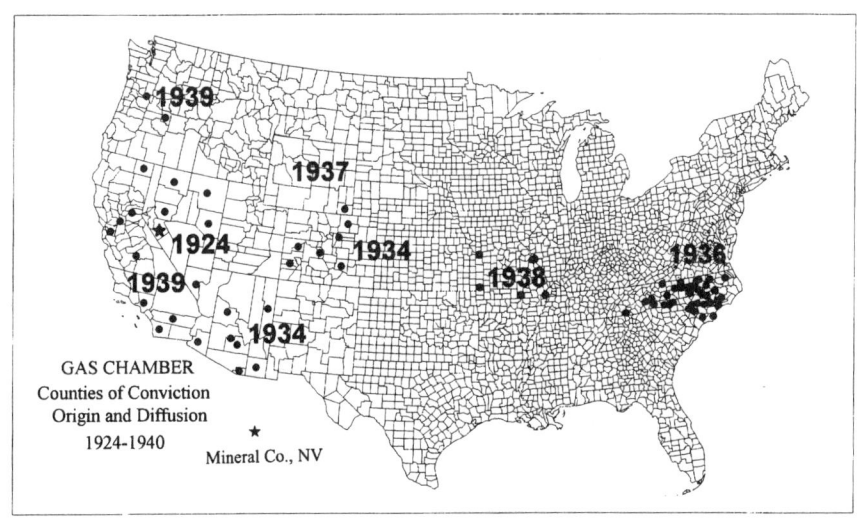

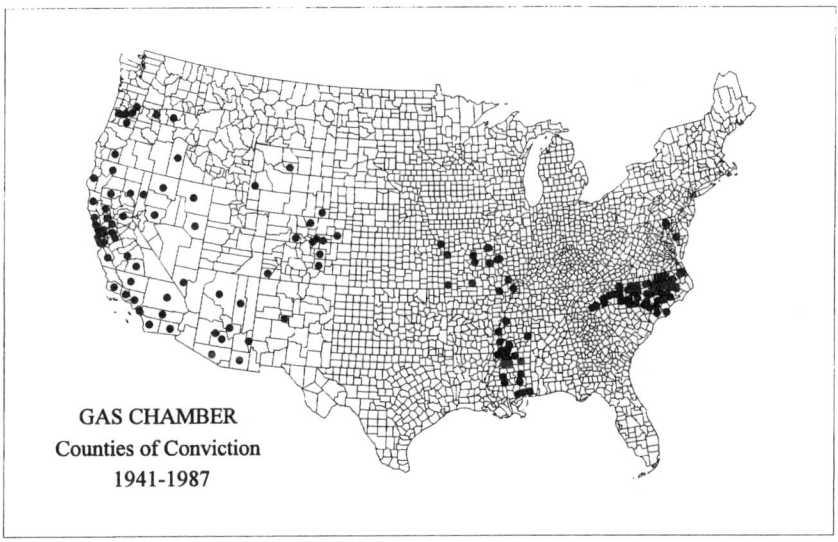

Figure 2.7. Origin and diffusion of the gas chamber.

Other Methods

Given that life is taken from everyone who is executed, it may seem odd that *methods* of execution could be controversial. This is the case, however, since not all methods of execution are equally effective, with effectiveness defined in terms of speed and certainty of death. In

1996, for example, Billy Bailey was hanged on 25 January in Smyrna, Delaware, having turned down the option of lethal injection. This event was the first hanging in Delaware in 50 years, and state correctional personnel had to go to Walla Walla, Washington, where hangings occurred in 1993 and 1994, to review technique. This review was supplemented by using U.S. Army documentation—hanging had not been legal in the Army since 1986, but the Army nevertheless was a repository of useful information on the subject. In theory, hanging should sever the spinal cord, resulting in a quick death, but in practice this is not necessarily the case, so that the offender may slowly die of strangulation. Prison officials were reportedly so worried about the Delaware execution that they felt it necessary to practice their moves for hours (Vick 1996a, 1996b). Hanging is legal in four states (Delaware, Montana, New Hampshire, and Washington), but until the Delaware event in 1996, only Washington had actually hanged anyone since 1976 (figure 2.8). Just as the Delaware hanging attracted hordes of foreign media, so had an execution by firing

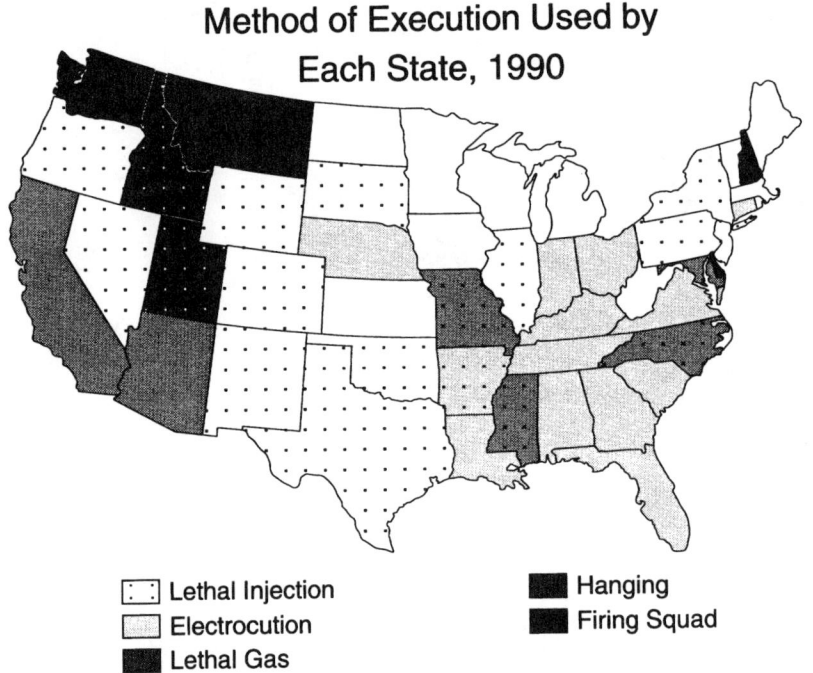

Figure 2.8. Methods of execution, by states. *Data source*: U.S. Department of Justice 1991a.

squad in Utah a few days earlier. (Idaho also retains the firing squad as an option.)

Recent Trends

The increased rate of execution since 1976 can be reviewed in light of contemporary trends in violent crime. In 1980, the homicide rate in the United States reached its highest level in the twentieth century, exceeding 10 incidents per 100,000 persons. This rate then declined through the early 1980s, only to start upward again in 1986, and by 1990 had reached a level almost equal to that of 1980 (Rand 1992). This increase was attributable in part to the emergence of the urban crack cocaine culture with its concomitant turf battles conducted with more effective weaponry. As lethal violent crime reescalated in the United States, public apprehension increased and policymakers came under renewed pressure to seek solutions. Public opinion polls often indicate that crime is most frequently mentioned as the greatest problem confronting the United States

The situation was exacerbated by the trend toward greater availability of more lethal firearms (e.g., Thomas 1992) and the evolution of new forms of violent crime such as drive-by shooting and car-jacking (e.g., Wilgoren 1992). The public's concern also increased with predatory attacks aimed at tourists as exemplified by heavily publicized robberies and murders of foreign tourists in the Miami, Florida, area. The attention given to the latter was ironic in light of the relative lack of attention given to "indigenous" violence; the latter had become so commonplace as to be relatively nonnewsworthy. For example, 1,208 homicides were recorded in Florida (128 of these in Miami) in 1992 (U.S. Department of Justice, FBI, 1993). Florida legislators became so concerned about the public perception of the impact of violence that proposed laws included the execution of 14-year-old murderers and the castration of rapists. The lawmakers described their constituents as "desperately afraid" and "worried that violent crime is not only eroding their lifestyles ... but threatening the state's economy ..." (Booth 1994, A3).

The enormity of the problem generated pressures for the stringent application of "control" measures: more and better-armed police, a national guard presence in certain neighborhoods, mandatory prison terms and more prisons, such special-purpose ameliorative measures as antidrug task forces, gun control in various forms, and even high-security fences at interstate highway rest stops to keep potential criminals from straying into adjacent neighborhoods. The advocates of control measures issued renewed calls for a broader-based activation of the death penalty, relatively little used since *Furman v. Georgia.*

Anecdotal evidence suggests that widespread fear of violent crime promotes the hope or belief that capital punishment will deter or at least provide the satisfaction of retribution;[4] this evidence comes from newspaper editorials, letters to the editor, radio and TV talk shows, casual conversations, and public opinion polls that probe the reasons for support of capital punishment.

Southern Emphasis

While some states, notably Texas and Virginia (Pressley 1992), have begun to execute residents of death rows after appeals processes run their course, use of the death penalty in the United States in recent decades has not only been quite limited, but has also tended to exhibit a southern emphasis in terms of number and rate of executions and of persons convicted to die. Ten of fifteen states that executed people in 1995 were southern[5] (figure 1.1). Of the 23 persons executed in 1990, 17 (74 percent) were in southern states, which were also overrepresented in terms of prisoners sentenced to death. By 1993, the total executed had grown to 38, with 28 (still 74 percent) from the South. Some 58.1 percent of the 2,356 prisoners on death rows in 1990 were found in the South (U.S. Department of Justice 1990), yet on a *per capita* basis only 34.3 percent would have been expected, based on a southern regional population of some 85.4 million out of a national total of 248.7 million (U.S. Bureau of the Census 1992). Using 1985 as a representative year, the South did indeed have a larger proportion of homicides than its population would predict (43 percent of the national total; U.S. Department of Justice, FBI, 1986, Table 3, p. 42), but both executions and death row populations in the South were still disproportionately large.[6] The southern emphasis prompted Von Drehle (1995) to refer to the region from Texas to Florida as the "death belt."

Various hypotheses, broadly divided into those featuring (a) economic and (b) cultural interpretations, have been advanced to explain this southern emphasis. Economic arguments see the South as a historically poor region prone to pathologies typical of poor societies. The cultural perspective views the South as having a different way of life, with relatively greater emphasis on personal honor, firearms ownership (in part a product of a more rural society), and child-rearing practices differing historically from those of the rest of the country. (For an extended literature review, see Harries 1990; Whitt *et al.* 1995.)

The Experience Since 1987

The last recorded execution in the Espy File was on 6 July, 1987. Between that date and 27 April, 1994, 154 executions took place (figure 2.9). In this period of approximately seven years, 79 percent of those events occurred in the South. While the *Economist* (1985) could note with respect to recent capital punishment that Florida was "the nation's undisputed execution leader," Texas subsequently far outstripped any other jurisdiction, with its 51 executions since 1987. Virginia (18) and Florida (17) followed. The contrast between South and non-South in terms of application of capital punishment also extended to method of execution, with the South using the electric chair for about half of its executions, and lethal injection for the other half. In the non-South, lethal injection was the overwhelming choice (81 percent), but the electric chair and hanging were used once each, and the gas chamber on four occasions.

The trend in very recent executions (through 1995) was decidedly erratic, far from the consistently upward linear trend that one might

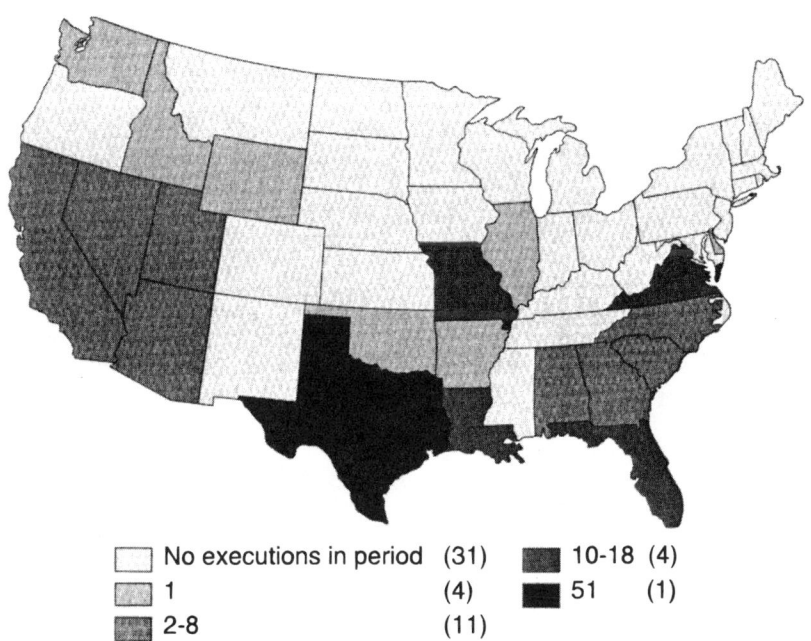

Figure 2.9. Executions, 8 July, 1987 through 27 April, 1994. *Data source*: National Coalition to Abolish the Death Penalty.

expect in light of public opinion and fear of violence. While executions did rise from 11 in 1988 to 16 in 1989 and to 23 in 1990, they fell back to 14 in 1991, rose to 31 in 1992, then up again to 38 in 1993, only to fall back to 31 in 1994. Data for 1995 suggested an upward spike with a total of 56, the highest since 1957. Again, Texas was the leader with 19, or 34 percent of the total, perhaps presaging a wave of executions as states fine-tuned their capital statutes to reduce the chances of technical error, and appeals ran out. However, regular predictions of "the floodgates opening" have, at least through 1994, proven to be premature (Associated Press 1996).

Homicide and Execution

Standardized Rates

Figure 2.10 shows trends in population-based homicide and execution rates for the United States between 1900 and 1985, expressed as standard (Z) scores with the mean equaling 0.0 and standard deviation

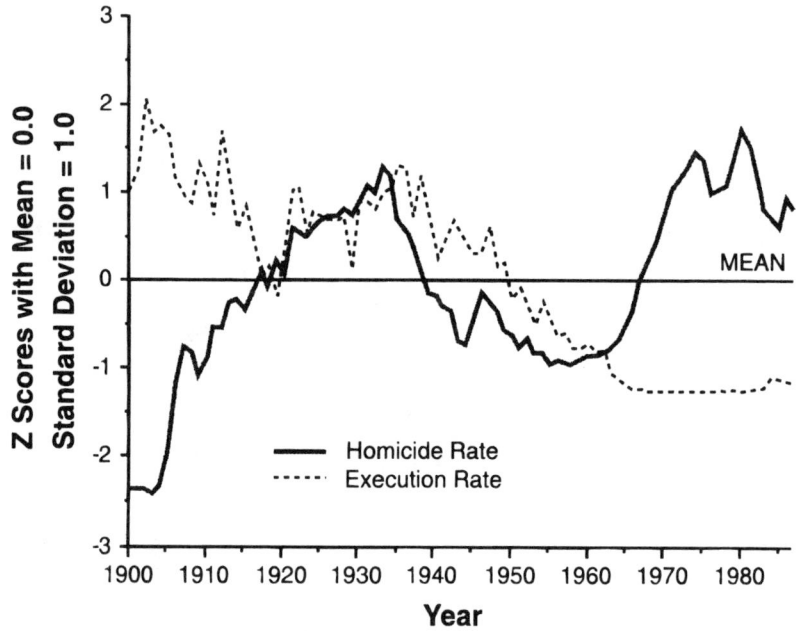

Figure 2.10. Homicide and execution rates, United States, 1900-1985. *Data sources*: Espy and Smykla 1987 (executions); National Center for Health Statistics, *Vital Statistics of the United States* [annual] (homicides); ICPSR (demographic data).

equaling 1.0.[7] The range of values, as scaled in figure 2.10, is between about 2.0 and −2.5, corresponding to an actual range in terms of homicide rates per 100,000 of 1.1 in 1903 (minimum) to 10.7 in 1980 (maximum). The execution rate range was between zero (several years) and 0.19/100,000, in 1902. If crude theoretical parity could be regarded as the situation that would arise if homicides and executions were to have the same population-adjusted rates,[8] the closest approach to this came early in the century when homicide rates were minimized and execution rates were maximized. At that time, around 1902–03, the execution rate was about one-sixth of the homicide rate. Given that more than 20,000 homicides can be expected annually in the 1990s, this would equate to some 3,300 executions, or about 17 times as many executions as have ever occurred in U.S. history in one year. However, the more representative *mean* execution rate has been around 0.05/100,000. This was exemplified by 1950, an average year, when the rate of execution was about 1 percent of parity. In contemporary terms, this would mean some 200–250 executions, comparable to the count in the peak years of the 1930s.

A note of caution is in order for figure 2.10. The curves have been rescaled in standard deviation units in order to provide a sense of how rates have varied with respect to their own means and standard deviations; the "real" rates, as noted above, differ substantially. Prudence would dictate that each curve is interpreted only in terms of trend (up or down) and with respect to its mean and variation. All that the two series have in common is that their means are both 0.0 and their standard deviations are 1.0 on the figure 2.10 scale.

Theoretically, the execution curve is a function of the homicide curve insofar as homicides are the (principal) crimes that "produce" executions. This production function varies greatly over time, with some correspondence in trends between the rates only in the period 1920–1960, when both curves were either rising together (about 1920–1940) or falling together (1940–1960). Between 1900 and 1920 rates were converging—execution rates downward, homicide rates upward. Between 1960 and 1980, homicide rates tended to rise while executions were more or less suspended. However, homicide rates also fell sharply while the execution hiatus was still operative.

Exploration of the historical pattern demands that one take into account the average time from conviction to execution: about seven years in recent decades. One should incorporate this lag into any analysis, shifting the execution curve to the left by seven years, so that execution(s) roughly correspond to the year in which the homicide(s) took place. While this lag is not presented graphically here, it would seem to offer little in the way of clarification.

Various interpretations could (and no doubt will) be drawn from this fragment of longitudinal data on the relationship between homicide and capital punishment. Proponents of execution could point to very low homicide rates when execution rates were highest (and maximally deterrent?) in the first decade of the century, as well as to rapidly increasing homicide when executions stopped. Opponents could point to quite high rates of both homicide and execution from about 1920 to about 1935, which tended to suggest that execution actually had little deterrent effect. In seeming to offer some encouragement to both opponents and proponents, these data in isolation ultimately provide no definitive help to either.

While the temporal dimension, at least in this context, is not particularly helpful in shedding light on the deterrent effect of capital punishment, prior analysis has suggested that interpretation based on territorial differences is more persuasive. States with historically high rates of execution have generally been those with high rates of homicide, predominantly located in the South. There, high homicide rates have been sustained independently of the rate of execution (see Harries 1985; 1988; 1990; 1992a). In an aggregate longitudinal interpretation such as figure 2.10, this regional dimension is necessarily submerged.

The generalized twentieth-century trend in the execution rate has been downward, while, much more ambiguously, that of homicide has been upward. Executions have declined relatively in part because of doubts about their utility, equity, and cost, culminating the *Furman v. Georgia* decision. That decision represented a turning point in the sense that the execution rate has not, to date, recovered to pre-Foreman levels. As the following discussion will demonstrate, states have also had difficulty passing capital statutes that are immune to technical challenges in the appeal process.

Examples of Regional Complexity: Maryland and Neighboring Virginia and the District of Columbia

Regional and Local Culture as the Key to Pattern

Regional and local cultures may have a profound effect on whether the death penalty even exists, and if it does, how evenly it is administered. In New Mexico, for example, where the law is on the books, zero executions have occurred in recent decades, perhaps owing to the opposition of the Catholic Church. In neighboring Texas, the *New York Times* noted that "the odds of a convicted killer's being put to death depend largely on where the crime took place . . ." (Lewin

1995). By early 1995, Texas had executed 92 people since the reintroduction of capital punishment, 37 of whom came from the Houston area, where the district attorney is a death penalty proponent. In contrast, only 5 came from Dallas, which has about two-thirds of the population of Houston.

In other states, too, executions occur unevenly with respect to what might be expected on the basis of the geography of capital offenses. This gives rise to intrastate "death belts." In Georgia, the contrast is between the central area where there were many, and the north, where there were few. (See also chapter 4 and Bowers and Pierce 1980a). In Tennessee, differences have been noted between Memphis and East Knoxville (many) and Nashville (few). As New York's new capital statute became operational in 1995, attention was drawn to the likelihood that the Manhattan district attorney would be unlikely to seek the death penalty owing to his opposition to it, while district attorneys in more conservative suburbs would be more likely to employ it. To some extent, the advocacy of capital punishment in any given case would depend on whether the case could be used by the district attorney as a stepping stone to higher office, as it was by Republican Congressman Steven C. LaTourette in Cleveland, Ohio. Prosecutorial discretion was also evident in two high-profile cases in 1995; the Susan Smith case in South Carolina and the O.J. Simpson trial in California. Smith, found guilty of drowning her two children, faced the death penalty, while Simpson, accused of murdering his ex-wife and her friend, did not (Lewin 1995; see also Verhovek 1995 and Eckholm 1995, for the *New York Times*'s analysis of the issues surrounding the reimposition of the death penalty in New York).

Maryland

Three political units, Maryland, Virginia, and Washington, D.C. make interesting case studies in the influence of regional culture and political process. Although these states[9] are neighbors, their recent capital punishment experiences are quite different. Maryland, in contrast to Virginia, had not, until 1995, executed anyone in more than three decades. This had not been for lack of capital convictions. Prior to 1995, the last execution in Maryland was that of Nathanial Lipscomb on 9 June, 1961, convicted of first-degree murder. In that year, in response to concerns about the breadth[10] of the Maryland capital punishment statute and the dearth of executions, the Murdy Committee on Capital Punishment was charged by the governor with reporting on the period 1936–61, during which 122 defendants (71 murderers and 51 rapists) were sentenced to death. Three principal findings emerged. First, some 60 percent of murders resulting in death sentences had victims who were strangers, and robbers or burglars who victimized strangers were most liable to receive the death penalty. Second, once sentenced to death, African-Americans were more likely to be executed, and third, as an occupational group, laborers were predominant among those receiving death sentences (State of Maryland 1993, 7).

In the 1960s, the National Association for the Advancement of Colored People aggressively attacked capital punishment, and executions gradually diminished until *Furman v. Georgia*, in which the U.S. Supreme Court found that it was the "unguided, standardless discretion allowed the sentencing authority"—arbitrary application—that made the death penalty unconstitutional; consequently, new capital punishment laws were enacted in 35 states in the period 1972–1976 (State of Maryland 1993, 8–9). A new Maryland statute followed in 1978 and divided the guilt-determination part of the trial from the sentencing part, incorporated consideration of aggravating and mitigating circumstances, and instituted automatic appellate review of any death sentence (State of Maryland 1993, 19).

Finding nine of the 1993 *Report of the Governor's Commission on the Death Penalty* found an uneven geography of capital prosecutions among the state's 24 "charging jurisdictions."[11] In each jurisdiction the commission reviewed the relationship between murder frequencies and the number of capital sentencing proceedings. It found that suburban counties with smaller populations were more likely to have capital sentencing proceedings compared to more urbanized areas. These differences were seen as being "primarily attributable to differences among the 24 jurisdictions' charging policies. . . . although the death penalty statute represents state policy, its application varies sharply . . ." (State of Maryland 1993, 200). The issue of possible racial disparity was more ambiguous. Public testimony before the Commission drew attention to the perceived unfairness of the death penalty, particularly the discriminatory effects of capital punishment on African-Americans, but the Commission found no such evidence while noting that this did not in itself prove or disprove the existence of discrimination (State of Maryland 1993:201).

Virginia

Virginia continues in its established role as a leading execution state, along with Texas,[12] Florida, and Louisiana, having put to death 23 persons since the restoration of the death penalty in 1976, and 6 in the 14-month period that ended in February, 1994, giving it the most "efficient" capital punishment system of any state; no other has executed such a high percentage of its death row inmates—over 20 percent (Baker 1994b; State of Maryland 1993). Given the active status of capital punishment in Virginia, the legislature has been involved in the adoption of execution changes, proposing lethal injection as an optional alternative to the electric chair (Baker and Babington 1994). Another proposal would permit the relatives of victims of capital offenders to view the execution, in order, in the words of one proponent, to achieve "closure" (Baker 1994a):

> Virginia's experience is different from [Maryland's], not only in assuring an expeditious review process, but in maintaining an exceptionally low reversal rate. That combination has produced over time a steady stream of executions. The low reversal rate may be attributable in part to the relative simplicity of Virginia's sentencing procedure; a simpler procedure produces fewer errors. . . . On the other hand, the low reversal rate in capital cases may reflect the effect of judicial elections on the legal culture of the Virginia courts. (State of Maryland 1993, 132)

The latter reference to judicial elections is significant. The popular election of judges could be construed as more likely to lead to the election of "hanging judges" in a climate of opinion calling vociferously for more frequent application of the death penalty. In Maryland, judges are initially appointed and then confirmed for continuation in office in general elections, a more indirect expression of public will. However, as this discussion suggests, neither interstate nor intrastate variations in capital punishment can be laid unambiguously at the door of any particular causal factor.

Washington, D.C.

Washington, D.C., like 12 states (see figure 1.1), has no death penalty. Although 118 executions have occurred as a result of capital convictions in the District, the last took place in 1957. Of the 118 executions (see table 2.1) 69 percent were of African-Americans. The most striking anomaly in the D.C. data is the year 1942, when more executions (eight) occurred than in any other. However, unlike the typical year in which all, or nearly all executions were for murders, the modal offenses in 1942 were the quintessential wartime crimes of spying and espionage, which accounted for six of the eight, all of white people. Interestingly, Washington, D.C. experienced extremely high rates of homicide in the 1980s and 1990s and yet resisted initiatives to reenact the death penalty despite its popularity with its neighbors, particularly Virginia.

Conclusion

The issue of capital punishment has intermittently surfaced in the media, and hence in public consciousness, in recent years. This renewed debate developed in response to concern over rising rates of urban violence and, the assumption went, the perceived need to crack down on offenders by stepping up executions in order to provide a deterrent. A subtext to this discussion related to the great cost of maintaining prisoners on death row through what the public has come to regard as the excessively lengthy appeals process.

Prior retrospective studies of capital punishment have mostly concentrated on analysis of the temporal dimension, although some research has demonstrated regional concentration, in the South, of high rates of both homicide and capital punishment. The research reported here extends prior work by developing general and specific *rates* of capital punishment in order to provide more meaningful temporal and geographic comparisons. Trends in homicide and execution since 1900 suggest a crude X model with generally rising homicide rates and generally declining rates of execution. However, these data are so ambiguous and limited that a conclusive case for or against capital punishment as a deterrent cannot be made solely on the basis of the temporal data. Rates of homicide have risen and fallen with capital punishment both present and absent. However, evidence comparing homicide rates with execution rates in a geographic framework fails to support the deterrence hypothesis, since states historically high in terms of execution have remained high in levels of homicide, whereas one would expect declining homicide rates if execution were a deterrent.

African-Americans have been heavily overrepresented in the process of capital punishment, both state-sanctioned and at the hands of lynch mobs, at least since nationhood, but data on violence are not adequate to the task of determining whether this actually reflected their greater involvement in violence in the early years of the republic. Certainly, in the second half of the twentieth century, the tragedy of disproportionate involvement of African-Americans in violence, both as victims and perpetrators, is all too apparent and will continue to be reflected in the demographics of capital punishment. Empirical data repeatedly point to the discriminatory implementation of capital punishment. (See: Bowers 1974, 1984; Gross and Mauro 1989, and Raspberry 1994, for extended discussions of the deterrence and discrimination issues.)

When scrutiny is more sharply focused on specific jurisdictions, a remarkable mosaic emerges made up of legal and cultural factors that bear on the form and function of capital punishment statutes. If a given state has a capital punishment statute (and 12, plus Washington, D.C. do not; see figure 1.1), the way in which judges are elected or appointed, local political vagaries as they relate to the likelihood of charges being brought or pressed against alleged offenders, and the complexity of the capital punishment statutes themselves are all relevant to the probability that more or fewer persons will be executed in a particular state. Legislatures constantly tinker with capital statutes. For example, Maryland excluded the mentally retarded from death sentences in 1989, and Virginia included armed robberies and attempted rapes in the definition of offenses qualifying as capital murders, also in 1989 (U.S. Department of Justice 1990). Presumably, such additions increase complexity and prospects for error at trial and concomitantly increase the chances of reversal on appeal. Insofar as all 51 legislative bodies can make such changes (including adding or removing capital punishment itself), it appears likely that capital punishment will remain a complex and controversial issue in the United States.

Notes

1. Interest in the possible deterrent effects of capital punishment continues, both in the popular media and the research community. See, for example, Cochran, Chamlin, and Seth (1994). Their research indicated that the reintroduction of capital punishment in Oklahoma produced no statistically significant reduction in homicide. However, stranger homicides increased.

2. Figure 2.1 includes all 14,570 cases.

3. Visually, large western counties, notably San Bernardino in California, are more obtrusive than their execution frequencies would warrant. This is merely an expression of the caveat that choropleth maps with variations in sizes of their statistical areas should be viewed cautiously.

4. A good example of a strong plea for exercise of the death penalty may be found in the *Baltimore Sun*, 22 September, 1992, which featured articles dealing with responses to the shooting of two Baltimore City police officers in the preceding week, part of an outbreak of firearm-related violence at public housing developments.

5. Federal government region definitions are used here unless otherwise indicated. Thus, the South consists of 15 states including Delaware, Maryland, and Oklahoma.

6. The issue of the *regional* relationship between homicide and execution is explored in more detail in Harries (1992a).

7. Execution rates were calculated by "attaching" execution frequencies in a given year to the decennial census population closest to that year. Thus, rates for 1915 through 1924 were based on the 1920 population of 106 million. Homicide rates were as published in official sources for each year. (See "Data sources" in the caption for Figure 2.10.)

8. This would happen if each homicide were to lead to an execution. While this is an absurd oversimplification, it provides a base for comparative purposes and a crude indication of how far from perfectly retributive the system has been in any given year in the twentieth century.

9. Although Washington, D.C. is not a state, it aspires to attain statehood and will be treated as a state for the purpose of this discussion.

10. Maryland law in 1961 provided for the death penalty for six separate offenses: assault with intent to rape, rape, carnal knowledge of a child under 14, kidnaping, kidnaping a child under 16, first-degree murder (State of Maryland 1993, 3).

11. These jurisdictions are the 23 counties plus Baltimore City.

12. The Virginia capital statute "closely resembles" the Texas statute. Texas leads in post-*Furman* executions with more than 60. Some observers have attributed this in part to the weakness of the public defender system in Texas (State of Maryland 1993, 131,136).

3

Capital Punishment and State Corrections Systems: Is There an Impending Crisis?

As of 31 August, 1995, 2,978 men and 50 women, a total of 3,028, awaited execution in the 38 states with provisions for capital punishment.[1] The pace of executions in the United States has increased since the end of the moratorium in 1977, but the increase appears as three distinct "plateaus" of execution levels (see figure 3.1). No more than five people were executed during any year between 1977 and 1983. Between 1984 and 1991, however, no fewer than 11, but never more than 25, were executed. Since 1992 at least 31 have been executed each year, with 56 executed in 1995. Moreover, we have been adding people under sentence of death to this list each year, with the number of new commitments varying from 159 in 1977 to 299 in 1987.[2]

At the same time, as noted in chapter 1, the past twenty years of public opinion in the United States has shown a definite shift in favor of capital punishment. Each year since 1982, over 70 percent of all people interviewed favored the death penalty for the crime of murder as one alternative in the criminal justice system. All of this—the increasing rate of commitments and executions, the increasing scope of the philosophical and moral debates as these figures increase, and changing public attitudes—will come to affect the correctional system. Indeed, it is so evident that this is true that policymakers seem to have overlooked serious consideration of what the effects may be.

Reality Check

It is not our intention in this chapter to reconsider the theoretical arguments regarding capital punishment, nor do we intend to address those studies that employ analyses of theory or empirical data in order

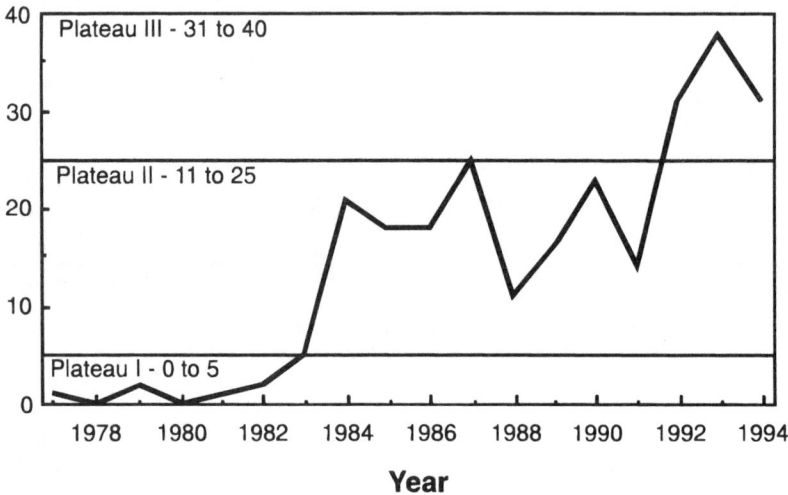

Figure 3.1. Three execution plateaus.

to test the efficacy of capital punishment as a deterrent or as an instrument of any other policy. Rather, we suggest that society must address these figures and their impact on the criminal justice system simply as an unavoidable reality that will affect us all profoundly. If society does not begin now to project where it is going and what may be expected on arrival, we will, as on many other occasions, be caught in a web of unintended consequences. Given the finality of capital punishment and the systemic and philosophical magnitude of the act for society, what appears to be a rapidly approaching crisis makes it particularly important to investigate this future scenario.

If, on 1 January, 1996, executions had begun at a rate of one person per day, six days a week year-round, it would be early in the year 2006 before we eliminated the present backlog of death row inmates. This, however, does not figure in the additional cases added each year that would have to be accommodated. Now assume that we add yearly increases at the current rate of commitments per year, minus a very liberal allowance for the questionable effects of deterrence (see the next section of this chapter). We would have to execute one person a day, six days a week, in order to eliminate the present backlog by sometime around January 2026.

However, experience with the changing nature of American public opinion and the effects of that opinion on legislatures and judicial agents leads to the belief that daily executions would produce a powerful backlash in public opinion, with a corresponding movement to reduce the number of executions. On the other hand, no matter how strong this public reaction might be, it seems unlikely that we could simply release all of these inmates or reduce their sentences without expecting a similar surge of opinion in the opposite direction.

Need to Inform Policy

Given these realities, social scientists should begin to use their experience and expertise to explore the logical alternatives that such an impasse may create in order to be in a position to inform policymakers on the possible effects of various alternatives. We will offer one scenario for corrections that seems quite plausible. It suggests that we may see the enactment of life-without-release statutes in most states (see also chapter 7) and the creation of supermaximum security facilities in some states to avoid large-scale executions, while avoiding the release of death row inmates back into the general prison population. We stress that it is not only this specific future vision that is important, however, but also the need for the social and policy sciences to begin to consider such visions.

The Pressure of Practical Numbers

Discounting legal arguments regarding constitutional and procedural aspects of capital punishment, the debate over the death penalty historically has focused on questions of the morality of the act or has employed empirical analyses to address the practical value of the penalty as a governmental policy. Researchers have analyzed both the morality of the act of state-sanctioned killing itself and the morality of the act as a necessary component of the system of justice. From Kant and Beccaria to van den Haag and Menninger, the issue has been repeatedly fought over common ground.[3]

Since the advent of modern social science, a major component of the argument has turned to the empirical investigation of the efficacy of capital punishment as either a deterrent or agent of moral or social retribution. Even these more "scientific" investigations, however, have a philosophical or metaphysical foundation that is dependent on the fundamental stance of the author. Most scholars seem to feel uneasy allowing the decision to kill to rest solely on a rational calculus of gain and loss devoid of a moral sense of right or wrong that would imply a predilection on the part of society one way or the other.

Imminent Crisis

We are approaching a crisis of action—a new dilemma—based upon the increasing numbers of inmates awaiting execution, numbers that will come to overwhelm the system, the public, and the media. It is a reality and a problem that we have virtually never faced before and that is now upon us.

The question is simple. *Are we really going to kill all the people we have on death row?*

Some of the scenarios that follow from answers to that question are so extreme that there is an initial tendency to discount them as unrealistic. Yet just as surely as people sit on death row, we must either follow through with our decision and kill them, or we must find some way to temper our actions and release some, if not all, from their sentences. If we actually begin to kill them at a rate necessary to keep pace with current sentencing, we are facing a bloodbath more extensive than our criminal justice system has produced in this century—perhaps ever. If we do not kill them, then we betray the sense of justice to society and to the victim that is implied in the enactment of the death penalty provision in the first place.

Both sides in the argument tend to agree on one point—that the death penalty is the most severe sanction we have to impose, the ultimate action of which a society is capable against one of its members. This fact argues against compromise, yet the magnitude of the effect of killing all those convicted or releasing them all mitigates against either of those raw options being put into effect. It is this dilemma, this paradox, that we are addressing.

Where Are We Now?

Figure 3.2 shows the number of death penalty commitments from 1977 to 1992 (dashed line) and the percentage change over that period (solid line). A projection of the commitment pattern clearly implies that we have reached a stable plateau in the number of people being sentenced to death in the United States. Since 1981 we have sentenced between 244 and 299 persons to death each year. A projection based upon the 1977 through 1992 commitments leads us to expect that if we continue to commit and execute at current rates, by the end of the century we will have nearly 4,000 individuals on death row. This assumes that the levels of commitment and of execution we have reached remain about the same. That, of course, is always a questionable assumption.

Consider this: If we had made projections based on both the levels and changes in the commitment rates and execution rates found between 1977 and 1983, we would have expected over 10,000 individ-

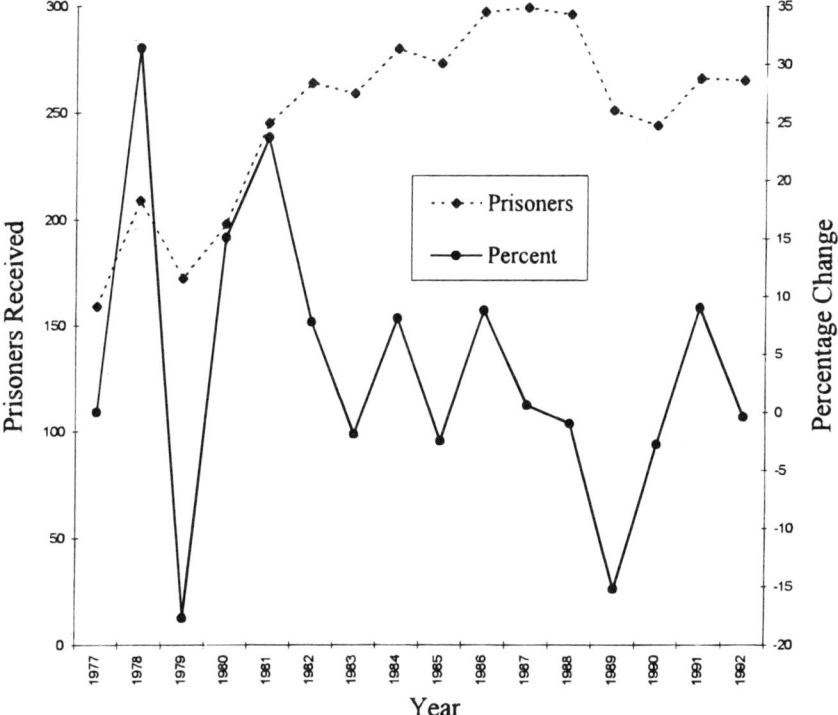

Figure 3.2. Prisoners received from court under sentence of death and percentage change from previous year—United States. *Data source: Sourcebook of Criminal Justice Statistics 1993.*

uals on death row by the end of the century. A projection based on the levels and changes in these rates from 1987 through 1990, on the other hand, would have predicted fewer than 3,000 on death row by the end of the century. In fact, we are currently executing around 35 a year on average and have already passed 3,000 on death row.

Projection Difficulties

In attempting to form some working assumptions, it is illogical to believe that we can use any set of available figures to generate accurate estimates of future patterns of death penalty commitments. Major internal and external attributes of the criminal justice system and the broader political structure are too numerous, too serious, too unpredictable, and change too quickly to enable us to use them as guidelines for projections. We must deal with the data we have on hand, and the most conservative reasonable estimate based on that data would be to assume that we have currently reached the plateau of commitments.

If the deterrence argument is correct, then capital crimes may decrease, and the need to execute will also decrease. The evidence for this is far too questionable to state it as a fact, but let us assume that each execution does, in fact, deter about eight homicides. If we begin by executing some 300 persons per year (one a day, six days a year with time off on Christmas, Easter, and other miscellaneous holidays), then we may prevent around 2,400 homicides, or about 12 percent of current totals. Again, these are assumptions based upon the best available data and, of necessity, ignore the accuracy of the data positing numbers of crimes prevented by executions, the theory behind such assumptions, and the sliding interrelated scales of crimes and executions as these change over time.

We have to assume that the percentages of murders and executions are proportional, so that we may expect for the near future a reduction in the commitment rate of 12 percent. But just to be on the safe side, let us double this estimate and assume a reduction of nearly 24 percent in the "necessary" execution rate, as manifested in the commitment rate. That would bring the number of persons sentenced to death to around 200 per year for the immediate future.

These, then, are our working figures. Some 3,028 individuals were under sentence of death in late 1995, and for the immediate future we will probably conservatively add around 200 persons per year to this number.

Option 1: Executions

If we continue as currently mandated and begin to execute, then there will be a series of systemic effects that will be problematic until the process of execution becomes routine. In most states, even if we begin to execute at a rate in keeping with sentencing, the currently existing system will not be strained to any great degree. Of these 38 states, 35 would probably be able to accommodate the executions within their current facilities, because in each of these states there are fewer than 100 individuals awaiting execution. Distributed over a period of 15 years, even with additions, this would amount to less than one execution a month.

The Big Three: California, Texas, Florida

But in at least three states, the numbers become so large that they may require significant change and expansion of the current system. As of 31 August, 1995, California had 418 persons awaiting execution,

Texas, 401, and Florida, 341. Three additional states, Illinois, North Carolina, and Pennsylvania, each have over 150 inmates on death row.

As we discuss each scenario and the potential external and internal effects, we will have to distinguish between the three large death row states and all others. In order to clear up their backlog and keep pace, each of these states will have to execute at a rate of one person each week for the immediate future once a steady program of executions is begun. Thus, just to keep pace *with these three states*, some 156 persons (roughly three times the 1995 national total) will have to be executed each year.

The Health and Welfare of Executioners

First, there is potentially a subtle problem of psychology and policy necessitated by employing a cadre of individuals capable of ending the lives of over 50 people a year on a regular and systematic basis for the foreseeable future. Although there would be no difficulty in finding such a staff, verifying the initial mental state and continuing mental stability of these individuals could be a delicate problem, despite the mechanical impersonality of the modern execution process. Beyond this, is the need to hold, process, and execute these inmates on a regular, systematic basis. All these technical details, however, are within the bureaucratic expertise of the correctional system. As past experience has shown, the system is generally capable of meeting the demands placed upon it.

What Happens When Executions are Commonplace?

Our newspapers would report on the daily executions, but the information would eventually no longer even make the front page once the level of executions reached over 300 persons a year, a number close to the record number of executions in the United States during the mid-1930s.[4] The number of executions in the United States would be greater than the number of murders in most Western European nations, and no Western industrial nation would have an execution rate approaching ours, in the unlikely event that any even retained capital punishment. The United States total would be closer to that of Iran or a number of Third World countries, nations often stereotyped by Americans as less than civilized.

What scant background and evidence we have to go on, then, suggests that the current cry for the death penalty would decrease and quite possibly reverse itself should we begin to execute at a rate commensurate with the demand we have created. If, in fact, we are wrong and public opinion *will* condone over 300 executions a year for over a decade and around 200 a year into the next century, then the United States will come to stand alone among Western industrialized nations, if it is not already doing so.

However, this volume of deaths at the hands of the state would, almost without doubt, initiate shifts in public opinion about the death penalty. Jolly and Sagarin (1984, 623) succinctly point out the paradox involved and reached the same conclusion.

> It is ironic that if the death penalty is not carried out with greater frequency, the cry can be raised that it is so unusual as to be capricious, arbitrary, and contrary to the Eighth Amendment; and that if it is increased in its frequency, the criteria for selection that marked the post-*Furman* era will not be able to be maintained. In either case, there is a possibility, violence and crime rates notwithstanding, that a new backlash against capital punishment may be forthcoming.

No conclusive evidence proves that such a backlash would occur, but several reasons lead us to believe that this would be the case. First, it is probable that much of the recent clamor for the death penalty reflects the rise in the crime rate from the early 1960s through the 1970s and the related increase in the fear of crime. Capital punishment has always been a ready and visible reaction to crime, one that seems to offer a certain and severe response of a nature proportionate to the violent crimes that produce the greatest fear on the part of the general public. It is, in short, probably not accidental that the increase in the crime rate and the increase in the percentage of people favoring the death penalty are positively correlated.

Yet in recent years the rate of crime has begun to show a decline, particularly the rate of general violent crime. If, as the literature suggests, the number of people favoring the death penalty is closely associated with rates of violence, we should expect to see decreasing percentages of people favoring the death penalty. An examination of the shift of public opinion on this issue presents evidence that great changes are possible in attitudes in relatively short periods of time. Only as recently as 1972 did slightly more than 50 percent of the population come to favor the death penalty for people convicted of murder, yet by 1983 that number had grown to 77 percent, and has remained above 70 percent to the present. (See also chapter 1.)

But if there is a new and powerful movement to cease or slow executions, what do we do with the people we have already sentenced?

To release these inmates sentenced to death or to change their sentence to a normal life sentence would threaten the underlying search for justice, security, or retribution that motivates the public to press for the use of execution. Systemically, such a change would probably have a negative effect upon morale of both employees and prisoners within the system. Further, it is difficult to calculate the effects of releasing into a general prison population a large number of offenders who had been under sentence of death. Although there are grounds to believe that the American people would resist the execution of 300 persons a year, there are also grounds to believe that they would resist just as strongly any attempt to treat these inmates under sentence of death in a fashion that would make them equivalent to any other offender.

It may be possible to return these offenders to the general inmate population in those states with only a dozen or so people on death row. However, we again consider those states that now hold a sizable population of offenders sentenced to death. Here the problem takes on a different dimension. So many inmates are involved that, even were the public to stand for it, the release of such a large number of inmates into the prison population of the state could produce considerable difficulties. Given their notoriety, the unquestionably violent nature of their offenses, the severity of their sentences, and the unique nature of their status, there is the danger that they would constitute a destabilizing influence in the inmate population of any state.

But more important, it would be politically impossible to simply commute the death sentences of these offenders into regular life sentences. Indeed, were the public to realize the loopholes in the most current "life-without-parole" statutes, even this option would not be acceptable.

As Flanagan (1982:83) has observed,

> Public approval of policy changes may be least likely when the offenders affected are long term prisoners, especially if the changes are perceived by citizens as presenting a greater risk to society of repeated victimization by these offenders or as representing leniency toward this group.

The public reaction to changes in status for inmates on death row would be even more serious, and there is virtually no reason to believe that the public would approve any policy that carried with it a possibility that these inmates might be released in the foreseeable future.

One option that does seem to avoid both the wholesale executions that could occur and simply changing the sentence of the offenders already on death row to a regular life sentence would be a "life-without-parole" sentence. It is possible that such a sentence, one that confines the offender for his or her life without chance of parole, commutation, release on good time, or any other release, would satisfy the sense of social and moral justice, yet would avoid the tension produced by excessive executions. As such, it might prove to be an acceptable compromise to the public. The idea of a genuine life-without-parole provision as an alternative to capital punishment is not new and has been discussed as a possible acceptable alternative both by opponents of the death penalty and at least one proponent of capital punishment (Yunker 1982, 123).

All of this is, of course, speculation based upon a series of "best estimates" and "most reasonable conclusions" from the data and our national history, and other scenarios are possible. However, the possibility is real that the public will balk at executing such a large number of people. The scenario envisioning the return of a large number of prisoners currently under sentence of death into an inmate population with life-without-release, life-without-parole, or other significant sanctions is a reasonable likelihood.

In considering the possible alternatives, one is logically drawn to look at the situation after the *Furman* decision required the release (or reclassification) of prisoners then under sentence of death into the general prison population. But two features make this case too different for worthwhile comparison. First, the numbers involved were smaller on a national level and at the level of each of the states. Second, *Furman* threw the issue of capital punishment itself into doubt. No one, including the prisoners, their lawyers, prison administrators, the public, or the lower courts knew what the subsequent status would be of capital punishment or of the persons previously or subsequently subject to the death penalty. Indeed, *Furman* probably increased pro-death penalty attitudes among the general public.

The impact of *Furman* was legal and structural, necessitating redefinition of the status of capital punishment. Now we face the results of those legislative changes, and our current crisis is pragmatic and immediate, reflecting the pressures and problems that we have created for ourselves.

Option 2: The Grim Prison of the Future

Prison Population Ecology

We have understood for decades that a prison is a delicately balanced social system—a negotiated, temporary peace between inmates, administration, and staff. The interjection of any factor that may disturb that balance has the potential to destroy the negotiated peace and threaten not only the status system of the inmate population but also the physical security of the institution and the staff. This is true whether the disturbing factor is intended as such, as in the case of agitators or gang warfare imported by new inmates into the institution, or whether the disturbing factor is as well intentioned as a "new" liberal administration. (See Irwin 1980, chap. 7, on the effects of "imported" street gangs; Jacobs 1977, chap. 4, for effects of administrative changes.)

The introduction of a sizable population of life-without-parole prisoners into the more traditional inmate population could have far-ranging consequences. Many of the standard sanctions, either positive or negative, normally used to maintain social control would be ineffective. Early release would not now be in the administrator's bag of benefits. One viable alternative is the creation of separate or segregated areas for ex–capital sentence prisoners. With this option, the sheer numbers of offenders come to determine the nature of the area. In states with large maximum-security facilities but medium-sized life-without-parole populations (over 35 but less than 100), a separate tier, wing, or building might prove adequate. In those states with larger numbers, over 100, a separate institution or separate facilities might have to be created to house them.

On the positive side of this alternative, we are not talking about a large number of states. There are currently 12 states with death row populations of over 100,[5] including the three states with death row populations over 300. In addition, we may assume that at least some of these inmates would remain on death row even if a life-without-release provision were to be enacted in all of the relevant states. It would seem, then, that only about 12 states would have to consider this type of institution, at least for the present. Of these states, at least five already have some variation on a life-without-parole sentence. The experiences of one of these states, California, are important in discussing these options and will be addressed later.

High Input, Low Output

Two factors give us pause with this optimistic assessment, however. First, we would be adding regularly to the population in these institutions. Normally, correctional systems attempt to maintain a population balance by releasing numbers of individuals at a rate roughly comparable to the numbers being brought in. But for the immediate future, prisons with this population would only increase (or would decrease at a minuscule rate through accidents, murders, suicides, and natural deaths). Pending some other change in our social system, public opinion, or the crime rate, we would find ourselves progressively adding states to the list of systems with prisons of this type. Those states that would already have such institutions would see them continue to grow at a rate proportional to the rate of capital punishment commitments.

Second, there is a natural tendency to use existing tools. If life-without-parole sentence becomes a viable alternative to the death penalty, we may reasonably expect that judges and juries will use it. Given its attractiveness compared to the finality of death, it will probably be used more extensively than we now find the death penalty employed. With more and more states facing the problems of institutions devoted to life-without-parole inmates, the problems of this type of prison and prisoner will be increasingly of national concern.

Problems

What sort of problems would the staff and administration face? What follows is a preliminary overview of some of the obvious features of this sort of institution. This list is neither complete nor more than a description of the problem. We are simply suggesting the direction for research and model-building that corrections systems should begin to consider as options for what seems to be a situation with some chance of occurring.

First, the staff would lose the controls that come from the possibility of early release. Not only would parole be out of the range of possibilities, but such standard mechanisms as "good time" (time off for good behavior) would disappear as well.

Second, the population would be qualitatively different from traditional prison populations. It would be a population reprieved from death. The dynamics of such a population are different from those normally encountered in a prison, in large part for the reasons listed below.

Third, this would be a population without hope of foreseeable release, one without a future on the outside. It is difficult to forecast what the effect of the reality of this cliche "without hope" would be on such a large and concentrated group. Theories abound on the effects we might expect, but they are a virtual smorgasbord. The frustration produced might create a suicidal fatalism, a stoic acceptance of reality, or a cauldron of violence in which neither staff nor other inmates would be safe.

Fourth, following this line of reasoning, one would encounter a population with, as the cliche would have it, nothing to lose. Undeniably, if a provision for capital punishment were to remain in state law, it could be used as the final threat and punishment for subsequent violent offenses within the institution. But having faced the death penalty before and "beaten" it, it is unlikely that it would serve as a serious deterrent for the individuals who make up this population.

Fifth, within decades, this would become a mixed-age population to a degree not encountered in normal prison populations. As the inmates became older, the normal pattern of release would not take place; older inmates who are simply waiting to die in prison would be confronted with young violent offenders. Such a mixture might prove to be a benefit, with the older inmates serving as a balance and mediating factor for the newer and younger inmates. However, the characteristics of these younger and violent offenders suggest that such a scenario is unlikely. Rather, this age mixture might be seen as a probable destabilizing influence.

Sixth, the institution may have a constant population. Turnover would be very low, and what did exist would never approximate the flow one sees in normal prisons.

Finally, the cost of such an institution would be staggering, particularly if it were constructed while simultaneously maintaining a system for capital punishment. As Nakell (1978) notes, the cost associated with the death penalty comes not so much from the specific costs of maintaining the prisoner and the execution chamber, but from maintaining the entire complex and necessary legal and procedural system. Were this cost to be borne in addition to the costs of building and maintaining the type of facility we have suggested, the burden on the taxpayer would be substantial. More than likely, the load would not be added to the taxpayer, but would be taken from the current budget of the state's department of corrections, draining the funds available for other institutions or programs to finance this institution.

This is not an exhaustive list of the problems in our hypothetical prison. It is intended not as a thorough description but as an initial indication of the more immediate, obvious, and troublesome aspects that we should expect. It is, then, a very grim and expensive prospect, a remarkably unpleasant setting. The inmate population would consist, without exception, of violent offenders. Indeed, it is likely that even the crime-of-passion murderers would be absent, so that the population would be the most problematic of even the violent offenders. Given the social correlates of these offenders, it would initially be a young population and, in most states, consist of urban minority youth often drawn from street gangs. The staff would have to be more vigilant and constantly on alert for the social, psychological, and physical nuances that would indicate the underlying structure and tensions of the inmate population and the institution itself. The same sort of demands would be present for the administration of this prison. It would require administration, organization, policy, and procedures that were constantly ahead of the majority of correctional establishments. In order to work at all, it would have to be a state-of-the-art maximum security institution.

The institution would have to be so constructed not simply because of the problematic nature of the inmate population but because of the public visibility of any problems that did occur. Any escape, disturbance, or homicide within this setting would generate extensive media coverage. The institution would be established as a "last resort" and would purport to be not merely secure, but so secure that inmates may as well have been executed for all the threat they pose to society. No leeway would exist for an occasional escape or for any flexibility in the demands made on staff, administration, or population.

Few state institutions approach this level of security or demand this rigidity. In the United States, the closest models may be the federal penitentiaries in Marion, Illinois, and in Florence, Colorado. Many of the states with larger inmate populations, as well as the federal prison system, have institutions that are recognized as the last stop for inmates within the system. For years, the U.S. Penitentiary at Marion has been such an institution, holding the "worst of the worst" inmates with an average sentence of 40 years as well as those who present management problems from other institutions in the federal system. Even there, the inmates have clear possibilities for progress and eventual release. If they perform well and abide by the regulations, they have the opportunity for transfer to less restrictive institutions or eventual release. Yet even this institution faces the realities indicated above.

Observations by Dean Leach, the executive assistant to the warden at Marion, highlight the problems. First, there is the need to maintain the death penalty even with the existence of such an institution.[6] As he noted,

> The inmates often don't care if they are caught if they kill you or assault you. We have had individuals assaulted and killed with impunity. There's nothing else we can do to them. We can get them another life sentence, but they are serving three or four already so what difference does it make?

Second, the obvious security problems are constantly present. "Any time you move a man it goes beyond normal bounds," Leach observed. "You can segregate the inmates, individual cells, individual recreation, but you can't mingle these people without problems." Yet, as the prison management was aware, any program that could totally protect staff and other inmates through the sort of segregation required would not only face a legal challenge but would be financially prohibitive.

The third factor, cost, is the traditional bottom line of corrections. In considering the sort of prison envisioned, the expense involved is well beyond the budget of most correctional systems. Indeed, it is reasonable to expect that most states would initially attempt to house these offenders in traditional facilities already in use. Administrators in institutions already housing large numbers of long-term violent offenders generally use traditional means of custody in a strict program designed by their administrative personnel. In these institutions, as in those housing less problematic populations, security is only as effective as staff and facilities can make it in day-to-day operation. In short, there are no reasons to expect the public to be willing to expend extremely large sums of money for the construction of the qualitatively different prison structures that would guarantee any measure of security beyond those that already exist.

Option 3: Operations as Normal

These predictions may be wrong; we could be overstating the impact of this group of former death-row inmates upon the system were they to be released into the general prison population. Some evidence supports this contention.

In his studies of long-term inmates, Flanagan (1980a; 1982) addressed the question of what correctional systems might do with offenders serving longer sentences. Many of his subjects were murderers, but Flanagan (1982, 83) observed that "the motives, justifications, and behaviors that are incorporated under the 'homicide' label are themselves of broad scope." Thus, although he was dealing with a group whose characteristics would unquestionably be more diverse than our hypothetical population, he also considered the two models that we have addressed, those of "dispersal" or "concentration" of offenders. He concluded that the "data presented argue in favor of the dispersal model" (Flanagan 1980a, 365).

California

In addition, California has over 400 persons on death row and has a life-without-parole statute, yet seems to have no problem with the dispersal of persons so sentenced in the general population of the prisons. The overwhelming impression of people involved with more serious offenders, both in California and in the federal system, is that there are no specific qualitative differences in security or custody procedures in dealing with these inmates.

Interviews with officials in California clearly indicate that the existence of this population of prisoners intermingled among other inmates does not pose serious, unique problems simply by virtue of the difference in the sentence. In the first place, even with this sentence, most of the inmates eventually are released from incarceration. By the time they are released, inmates tend to be far older and have spent substantially more time in prison than "normal" prisoners. But the state, as one official observed, does not like to have people die in prison, and even with these inmates there will be some sort of commutation as they reach old age (or late middle age).[7]

More directly, a correctional official pointed out that "people have got to live. Thinking about what is going to happen 12 years or more from now is a mere fantasy. They deal with what is here. We don't think they deal with their sentence in any way that is different from a normal lifer."[8] At that, their experience of incarceration will not be substantially different from individuals serving sentences with possibility of parole.

Although this experience indicates that there are no substantially different problems with the life-without-parole inmates and others, the changing nature of the characteristics of serious offenders may have some impact. California authorities have found, as have officials in other states, that when younger, often gang-affiliated offenders come into the prison population, the extent of the violence problem increases. However, we must be careful not to overestimate the effect of this changing population upon institutions, given our inadequacies in separating specific causes from effects.

We are well advised, then, to look to the case of California and the information from other sources on long-term prisoners in making predictions. There are unique conditions in California that might not be representative of typical cases encountered in other states were they to enact a life-without-release statute and attempt integration of the death row population into their prisons.

First, California is large enough to allow it to separate gangs or other factions among eight maximum-security facilities. Other, smaller states might not have this luxury. By the same token, gangs may serve as resources for integrating individuals into stable inside lives and may provide the personal and social support missing for most long-term inmates. Smaller states might find that there are no stable groups already in institutions into which newly integrated life-without-release inmates might fit. On the other hand, they might find that the existence of such groups provides a battleground for the continuation of conflicts imported from the streets and adopted by these new inmates.

Second, the provisions for life-without-parole and the death penalty have coexisted and have been in use in California over time. The creation and use of such a sanction would constitute a new policy in other states, and its enactment would introduce *en masse* a qualitatively different inmate subgroup into the population. Those states that have not had a tradition of life-without-parole inmates in any substantial numbers would encounter the problem in one direct confrontation, with no gradual adjustment on the part of the other inmates, the administration, or the staff.

Third, some evidence suggests that we are encountering an increase in particular types of homicide offenders, specifically younger offenders involved in stranger-to-stranger, felony, or gang homicides rather than the traditional "crime of passion" murders that were the norm until the past decade (see Cheatwood 1990; Decker 1993). If this population is overrepresented in the population now on death row, which would seem to be a logical assumption, we would be dealing with a younger population with far less empathy and a far more violent character than may have been the case with the normal life-without-parole population in California.

We have not addressed some issues and questions, and we may have erred in our assumptions or in the conclusions drawn from them. However, if most of the assumptions are correct, then the dilemma suggested for corrections in the near future should be considered while there is time to mull over alternatives.

Even if we are wrong in our specific conclusions regarding the impact of changes in capital punishment on corrections, there is too much evidence on the vagaries of public opinion to believe that we are substantially in error in our predictions of reactions to increased use of the death penalty. At the least, then, corrections systems should begin to consider the possible nature of these major changes in public opinion.

Summary and Conclusion

Currently, the philosophical debate on capital punishment cannot be resolved. There is anything but agreement on the empirical debate over the effects of capital punishment, and virtually no historical, philosophical, or scientific evidence leads us to believe such a resolution will occur in the United States in the twentieth century.

Faced with the problem of increasing death row populations and the probability of strong public reaction to a large number of executions, life-without-release statutes seem to be an obvious option for a number of states. This is a guess based upon a series of assumptions given current data, a familiarity with the history and current status of the criminal justice system, and an awareness of the history and ongoing reality of the political system in the United States. We have been a nation built on compromises and mutual negotiations of conflict. If we continue to be so, then the most likely outcome is a compromise on this issue, rather than a total policy victory by either side.

The polar options of executing all the death row inmates or of releasing them all from prison seem to be so extreme on their face that, were either of them to be enacted, we can only envision a public opinion response so strong it would force the political and criminal justice systems toward the other extreme. Although this sort of opinion pendulum is common, we find that on most issues the pendulum seems to obey some sort of social law corresponding to natural law and comes to rest near the center—at least until some other outside force comes to act upon it and send it into motion again. Thus, attempting to execute the full population on death row and the additions to the population that will come in the next few years will strain the credibility of even the most hard-line proponents of the death penalty. Yet releasing all of these people into the general prison population would create a public furor, and releasing some of them, no matter how selectively, could produce a legal, administrative, and constitutional nightmare.

One possible outcome is a compromise resulting in an isolated section of life-without-release inmates in the correctional system of the states retaining the death penalty. In some states the small number of such inmates, the sparse budgets of correctional agencies, and the high cost per inmate of supermaximum facilities will necessitate the integration of life-without-release prisoners into the general populations of maximum-security facilities. In other states, separate tiers, sections, or wings of current facilities can be set aside for this population. And finally, it appears that in some states the sheer volume of these prisoners could necessitate a separate institution.

None of these are good alternatives. However, they are situations to which we should begin to pay close attention, because sentencing patterns imply that they may become a pressing and unavoidable reality sooner than we will be prepared to deal with them.

Notes

1. The source for this statistic is *Death Row, USA*, a publication of the NAACP Legal Defense and Educational Fund, New York, and constitutes the best current count of individuals on death row as of that time.

2. Based on data available through 1992.

3. For a comprehensive review of the empirical findings and theoretical and moral debates, see the following special issues: the *Yale Law Journal* (1975, vol. 85); the *Criminal Law Bulletin* (1978, vol. 14, no. 1); and *Crime and Delinquency* (1980, vol. 26, no. 4). The texts by Sellin (1967), Bedau (1982), and van den Haag and Conrad (1983) also contain excellent reviews.

4. On 29 February 1983, the 13th execution since 1977 occurred when J. D. Taylor Jr. was executed in Louisiana. The execution did not make the NBC morning news nor the front page of the *Baltimore Sun*. In 1995, routine executions in Texas did not regularly make the front pages—nor even necessarily the front sections—of major papers in that state.

5. The states are California, Florida, Texas (the big three), Alabama, Arizona, Georgia, Illinois, North Carolina, Ohio, Oklahoma, Pennsylvania, and Tennessee.

6. The interview with Dean Leach of the United States Penitentiary at Marion was conducted in February 1984.

7. Without exception, individuals interviewed from the attorney general's office of each of the states with life-without-parole provisions perceived that the actual operation of the system could countermand the intent of the statute. Through pardons and clemency, life-without-parole inmates can also expect release in some states.

8. Questions regarding the California case were taken from an interview with Robert Dickover, research program specialist for the California Department of Corrections, February 1984.

4

The Geography of Capital Punishment and Homicide: Regions of Violence

In this chapter, we develop an informal test of the long-term deterrent effects of execution through analysis of the relationship, if any, between regional patterns of violence that capital punishment is nominally intended to deter and patterns of the capital punishment response. Capital punishment has long been regarded as the first line of defense against such violence. It has found application throughout history in response to a variety of behaviors that the mores of the moment dictated as deserving the ultimate penalty. In the current sociopolitical environment, faith has been renewed in capital punishment as a multipurpose tool.

First, and perhaps foremost, it is a political panacea to prove that members of legislatures, state and federal alike, have "done something" about violence. Second, it is held up as a deterrent that will actually change human behavior. Third, it permits victims' families some measure of satisfaction through retribution. Finally, it is the ultimate incapacitation: people executed will not repeat their crimes, just as those executed in error will never complain.

Legislation produced by the 103rd and 104th United States Congresses illustrated the (political) importance of shortening the appeals process for capital offenders and of increasing the number of offenses eligible for the death penalty. The Crime Control Act of 1993, Section 706, "Federal Death Penalties," for example, changed the wording in some federal criminal statutes from "shall be subject to imprisonment for any term of years or for life" to "shall be *punished by death* or imprisonment for any term of years or for life." While this change will have very little practical effect, it permits politicians to show that they have greatly increased the number of death-eligible crimes, at least on paper.

Just as attitudes toward crime and punishment vary with time, they also vary sharply in space. For every peak or valley of punitiveness over time is an analogous peak or valley in geographic space. A more subtle aspect of punitiveness was brought out by *The National Survey of Crime Severity* (Wolfgang et al. 1985), which implied that high rates of homicide and execution over extended time periods may have something to do with what appears on the surface to be a lesser level of concern about loss of life in some locations compared to others. Thus, relatively frequent executions may reflect a degree of indifference toward life (or at least the offenders' lives) rather than a rabid "hang em high" attitude—or perhaps some combination of the two.

Regional Cultures

Crime control, like crime itself, has distinctive regional flavors, with regional cultural values reflected quite effectively in the legislative process, as illustrated in struggles over handgun control in the U.S. Congress in 1988 and 1991. Capital punishment shares in this regional distinctiveness, states' rights having allowed the states to decide both whether they would have capital punishment at all and, if so, what methods would be used to carry it out.[1] Federal oversight has been limited to the test of whether state laws have been constitutional. The *Furman v. Georgia* case determined that capital punishment was not being administered in an equitable manner, compelling a redrafting of state laws and effecting a moratorium on capital punishment between 1967 and 1977. Not surprisingly, when the states were thus compelled to reinvent capital punishment, they did so with considerable variation, as illustrated in chapter 2.

Precursors

Southern Violence Construct

One of the most enduring generalizations in the social geography of the United States is the prevalence of high rates of violence in the South (e.g. Brearly 1932; Lottier 1938; Harries 1971, 1985; Messner 1983a, 1983b; Huff-Corzine et al. 1991; Whitt, Corzine, and Huff-Corzine 1995).[2] However, the specific issue of the relationship between homicide and capital punishment has never been examined in a geographic context, although the question was broached in a preliminary investigation of the relationship between the geographies of homicide, capital punishment, and perceived crime severity (see Harries 1988).

Until recently, no data base has been adequate to an in-depth investigation of the geography of execution, although homicide data have been available in Federal Bureau of Investigation sources or vital statistics compilations for at least half a century. The present discussion draws on the literature of regional interpretations of homicide for a model of homicide geography to act as a paradigm within which to examine the geography of the corollary of homicide, capital punishment (Harries 1985). The latter analysis examined per capita homicide rates by states for nine five-year periods, 1935–80. The rates were treated both as state means across the quinquennia and also generalized into a map designating five violence regions: *very high*, *high*, *intermediate*, *low*, and *highly variable*. (The latter consisted of only one state, Nevada, which has been absorbed into the "high" category for the purpose of the present analysis.) All states classified as "high" or "very high" in this longitudinal profile were in the South, as predicted by the literature.

Data Base

The data archive utilized for this analysis is again the Espy File, which has been used for several other analyses in this book (Espy and Smykla 1987). For the purpose of this analysis, only data applicable to the period 1 January 1930 through 6 July 1987, were included. This 57.5-year period was selected for approximate congruency with the study period employed in the parallel 1935–80 analysis of homicide in the United States from which the violence regions employed here were derived. The study period coincides with capital punishment eras identified by Schneider and Smykla (1991) as "peak" (1930–39) and "decline" (1940–87).

Based on preliminary analysis of the structure of data for the time period under review, variables were collapsed into a few theoretically consistent categories in order to facilitate correspondence analysis (see note 6). Seven race codes were collapsed to four, age was reduced to three, crime to two, and the 743 occupation codes were reduced to "professional" and "other." Thus, the data matrix was expressed as 13 execution attributes against 4 regions, for 52 matrix elements across a raw base of 3,961 events.[3]

Research Question

Capital punishment has become narrower in focus over time, with execution, since 1976, reserved mostly for felony murders, that is, murders occurring in the commission of other crimes, such as rape-murders and robbery-murders (Peterson and Bailey 1991).[4] However, the general homicide rate is regarded here as a surrogate for capital homicide in that overall rates of serious violence are adequately represented by the underlying homicide regions used as a frame of reference.

Given that prior research identified robust homicide regions for the post-1930 period, the general research question is framed as follows: *Is the geography of execution a reflection of the geography of homicide?* This general question is approached at two levels: 1) analysis of the relationship between execution rates and homicide rates, and 2) an examination of the relationship between the homicide regionalization and generalized execution attributes. Do the characteristics of people executed, the crimes they committed, and the execution methods employed relate in any systematic way to the underlying pattern of related offense generalization?

Systematic variations in capital punishment between homicide regions would imply the possibility of the existence of regional cultures of capital punishment, analogous to the regional cultures of homicide suggested, for example, by Messner (1983). While the existence of such regional cultures of violence has never been conclusively established, and signs of violent regional cultures have tended to disappear when underlying socioeconomic conditions have been controlled for, the existence of general cultural differences across the United States has not been questioned, and available evidence indicates that it is indeed likely that regional predilections for discrimination exist, expressed in terms of attributes of inmates executed and methods of execution.

Inter- and Intrastate Variations in Capital Punishment

This contention is supported quite strongly, for example, by Bowers and Pierce (1980a), whose detailed analysis of death sentences based on data gathered in the late 1970s found that capital punishment varied significantly both between and within states. At the interstate level, they showed that a death sentence was more likely in Florida and Georgia than in Texas, for both felony and nonfelony murders, an observation that the authors noted could be attributed to "legally relevant variations" (p. 601).

However, their analysis of intrastate variations, where differences in state law no longer applied, showed that a death sentence was much more likely in the panhandle of North Florida compared to South Florida, by a factor of about 2.5. Larger variation was seen in Georgia. It was more than six times as likely that a death sentence would be handed down in the central part of the state compared to the northern, and between seven and eight times as likely compared to the Atlanta area. Bowers and Pierce estimated that the probabilities of such differences occurring by chance were 2 in 1,000 for Florida and 1 in 1,000,000 in Georgia.[5] (See also Gross and Mauro 1989, and chapters 2 and 5 of this book.)

Methods

First, state- and regional-level relationships between rates of execution and rates of homicide were investigated using map comparisons and correlation and regression analyses.

Second, correspondence analysis was employed to permit visualization of execution attributes seen in what might be called "homicide region space." Correspondence analysis allows the generalized representation of categorical data in a few dimensions (two, in this study) in which *graphic* proximity represents *statistical* proximity.[6] Thus, when homicide regions are located in category space, the relationship between execution attributes and homicide regions can be seen at a glance.

The locations of variables in the two dimensions are an analytical function of chi-square values derived from frequency tables. Points close to the origin[7] (see figure 4.2 below) contributed approximately zero to the total chi-square value for the underlying contingency table. Such variables also contributed little or nothing to *inertia*, which in correspondence analysis is analogous to the concept of variance in principal components analysis (SAS Institute 1989). While correspondence analysis is a descriptive technique among the class of methods generally referred to as *exploratory data analysis* and is not usually used for hypothesis testing, it is nevertheless versatile and flexible (Hoffman and Franke 1986). The method is particularly useful in applications such as the present one, in which an effort is made to understand relationships in a large matrix of categorical data.

Analysis

Relationships Between Execution Rates and Homicide Rates

As a preliminary step, a map was constructed to show population-adjusted standardized execution rates, by state, superimposed over the homicide regions derived from earlier research (Figure 4.1). The map permits a preliminary assessment of the relationship between rates of homicide and rates of execution and illustrates the focus of high rates

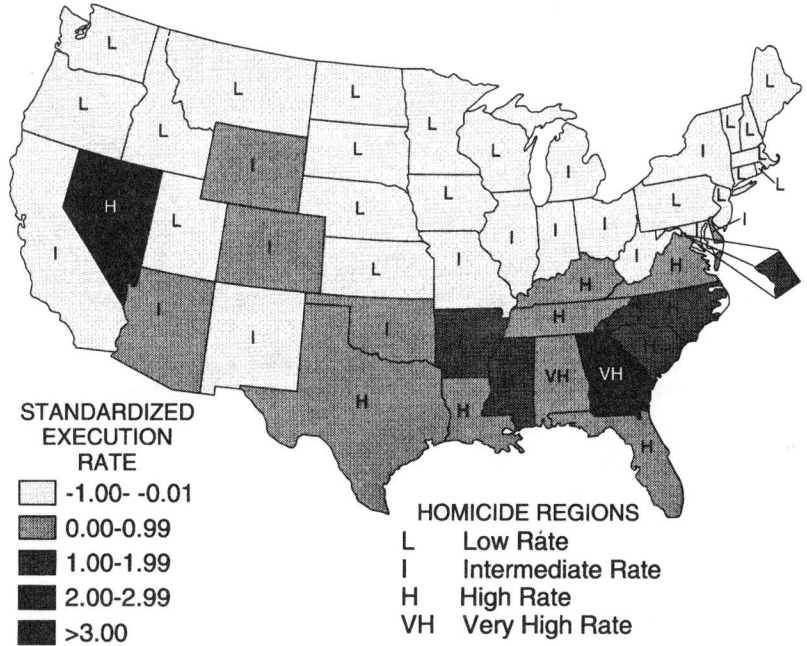

Figure 4.1. Population-based execution rates expressed as standard scores with mean 0.0 and standard deviation 1.0, and homicide regions. *Source*: authors.

of both execution and homicide in the South. Indeed, no states of the deep South are found below the mean, and, with the sole exception of Nevada, all states with scores above 1.0 are southern (including the District of Columbia). The two states classified as "very high" in the underlying homicide regionalization, Alabama and Georgia, were also high in execution rate; Georgia ranked second overall, Alabama ninth. All states classified as "high" in the homicide taxonomy were above the mean execution rate. The five zero-execution states were among states classified as "low" in the homicide scheme. Thus, simple map comparison suggests a clear positive correlation between homicide and execution rates, confirmed by the calculation of a correlation coefficient ($r = 0.55$, $p < 0.01$). Regression of the state-level execution rate on the homicide rate yielded extreme positive residuals for a group of southern states including, in descending order, Georgia, Mississippi, South Carolina, Arkansas, North Carolina, and Louisiana. Ranked extreme negative residuals were: New Mexico, Tennessee, South Dakota, Alabama, Florida, and Michigan.

Regression analysis also suggested the robustness of the a priori homicide regions, in that the homicide rate was not significant with region controlled (F = 15.23, p < 0.01). In the former group, execution rates were much higher than the respective homicide rates would predict, in the latter group, much lower. Alabama, Florida, and perhaps Tennessee would appear to be anomalies in that they would not be expected to appear in the negative residual group. Among these states, Alabama's mean homicide rate—at 8.90/100,000 the highest among the states—was 3.22 standard deviations above its mean. While the state also experienced an execution rate (4.32/100,000) almost 1 standard deviation above the mean rate of 2.61, it was not high enough to prevent a negative residual. Georgia, by comparison, had a homicide rate of 5.00/100,000, but an execution rate of 9.61/100,000, 3.23 standard deviations above that mean.

Correspondence Analysis

The analysis provided a useful graphic representation of the structure underlying the data, particularly with respect to the relationship between the violence regions and offender attributes (figure 4.2). As

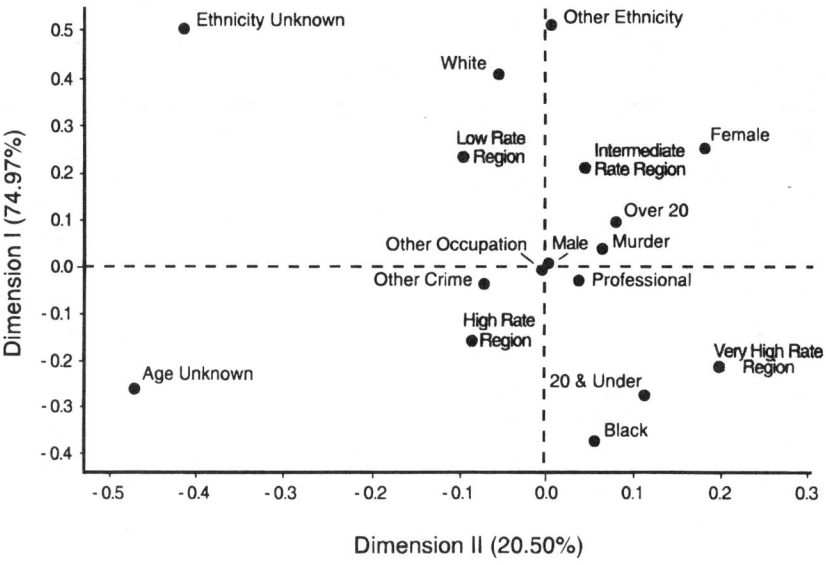

Figure 4.2. Execution attributes in the context of homicide regions, expressed in two dimensions. *Source*: authors.

noted above, the data are represented in two dimensions, of which dimension 1 accounted for 75.0 percent of the total chi-square and inertia, and dimension 2, 20.5 percent. A third dimension, accounting for only 4.5 percent, was omitted. Dimension 1 represents levels of homicide, with lower rates toward the top and higher toward the bottom. Most striking, perhaps, is the proximity of "black" and "20 and under" descriptors to the higher-rate regions and the location of "white" in the vicinity of the lower-rate areas. Some examples will help convey a sense of how points are located on the diagram.

In the two high-violence regions, the observed frequency of African-Americans executed far exceeded that expected, based on normal chi-square calculations using marginal totals to determine expectations; the reverse was true in the two low-violence regions, with the largest contribution to overall chi-square coming from the discrepancy in the "intermediate" region. In sum, "black" contributed 310.7 to total chi-square, or 32 percent of the total of 979.1 (table 4.1). This pattern is similar to that of "20 and under," which is located in the same general area of figure 4.2[8] It is also the mirror image of the pattern for "white" (which was overpredicted in lower homicide areas and underestimated in high-rate regions), itself comparable to the structure of "other ethnicity." Thus, the latter two variables, with homicide characteristics essentially the inverse of "black" and "20 and under," fall at the opposite, low-violence end of dimension 1.

Table 4.1. Contributions of two variables illustrating high (black) and low (male) chi-square values in the correspondence analysis.*[1]

Violence Region	Observed		Expected		Obs. Exp.		Chi-square[2]	
	Black	Male	Black	Male	Black	Male	Black	Male
Very high	424	516	270.6	515.7	153.4	0.3	87.0	0.0
High	1047	1556	814.3	1552.0	232.7	4.0	66.5	0.0
Intermediate	468	1380	726.9	1385.4	-258.9	-5.4	92.2	0.0
Low	122	476	249.2	475.0	-127.2	1.0	65.0	0.0

* Source: Data source Espy File, calculations by authors (see note 6).
[1] All values rounded to the first decimal place.
[2] Total chi-square = 979.1.

Table 4.2. Total chi-square values and associated inertias.*

Variable	Chi-sq.	Inertia
Age 20 and under	34.0	0.03
Age over 20	41.4	0.04
Age unknown	177.4	0.18
Murder	11.0	0.01
Other crime	11.0	0.01
Professional	0.8	0.00
Other occupation	0.0	0.00
White	282.6	0.29
Black	310.7	0.32
Other ethnicity	55.5	0.06
Ethnicity unknown	50.7	0.05
Male	0.0	0.00
Female	4.0	0.00

Source: Calculations by author.
*For more explanation of the inertia concept, see appendix III.

Variables such as "male" and "other occupation," on the other hand, contributed little or nothing to total chi-square, owing to the similarity between their observed and expected frequencies within murder regions (tables 4.1 and 4.2). Thus, these variables are located in "neutral" territory in figure 4.2, scoring about zero on both dimensions, indicating that they were structurally unconnected to either higher or lower homicide rate regions. This may seem counterintuitive in that it is well known that the overwhelming majority of homicides are committed by males.[9] However, this fact applies similarly to *both* higher and lower homicide rate regions; hence, it is neutral in terms of the display of structure in figure 4.2.

Conclusion

The evidence presented here suggests that, in very general terms, homicide regions are reasonable surrogates for the regionalization of capital punishment insofar as they permit discrimination in terms of certain attributes of executions and persons executed, within the reference period. Analysis, including comparisons of indices and the graphic representation of categorical data, reinforced the concept of disproportionate involvement of youthful minority people in violence and its concomitant punishment and, in concert with findings from related research, provides some support for the concept of discrete regional cultures of capital punishment.

If capital punishment were a significant deterrent to homicide, a sharply inverse relationship should appear between the two phenomena, particularly when seen in longitudinal perspective. That high homicide rates and high execution rates are strongly *positively* correlated does little to advance the deterrence argument.

Demographic and legal factors notwithstanding, the general temporal persistence of excessive minority/youth involvement in capital offenses in high violence regions (and in inner cities in general) is indicative of deep-seated problems in social structure. Endemic discrimination, expressed through the low socioeconomic status (SES) of African-Americans, is clearly reflected in their lopsided involvement in violent crimes. Thus, in the foreseeable future, African-Americans will continue to contribute disproportionately to the pool of persons susceptible to capital punishment. This general social imbalance, in concert with the regional variations illustrated here, presents a formidable, if not insurmountable challenge to policymakers.

Notes

1. Echoing in a bizarre way the new interest in the ancient practice of execution, the states of Delaware, Montana, and Washington still allowed the archaic and unreliable technique of hanging, and a prisoner was scheduled to hang in Delaware in the summer of 1991 (Heine 1991). There, James W. Riley had a choice between hanging or lethal injection (introduced in 1986). However, in exercising his right to refuse to choose, Riley was to automatically go to the gallows, under Delaware law. In the period 1930–87, less than 13 percent of executions in the United States were hangings, and the frequency of hangings declined steadily after 1930. Seventy percent of all the prisoners hanged in the period were executed in the decade of the 1930s. Adherence to hanging should be seen in the context of the availability of lethal injection technology. (See also chapter 2).

2. Theoretical constructs to explain the focus of violence in the South remain ambiguous, with two principal lines of argument, one relying on mea-

sures of poverty, the other on cultural factors. Exploration of the issue is beyond the scope of this paper; the reader is referred to Harries (1990) and Huff-Corzine et al. (1991) for extensive reviews.

3. The proportion of convictions actually carried out, a possible measure of the punitiveness of a culture, was not evaluated here. The data base addressed only actual executions. Furthermore, this measure would be confounded in practice by such rulings as *Furman v. Georgia*, effectively emptying death rows at a particular point in time.

4. 1976 is the key date due to a U.S. Supreme Court decision in that year, *Gregg v. Georgia* (Peterson and Bailey 1991).

5. Bowers and Pierce (1980a) were concerned primarily with issues surrounding capital sentencing in the wake of the *Furman* decision ruling existing state capital statutes unconstitutional. They concluded that "differential treatment by race of offender and victim has been shown to persist post-*Furman* to a degree comparable in magnitude and pattern to the pre-*Furman* period" (p. 629).

6. Correspondence analysis is also known as dual scaling, optimal scaling, canonical analysis of contingency tables, homogeneity analysis, categorical discriminant analysis, and other labels. According to Hoffman and Franke (1986), three conditions should be satisfied for the effective application of correspondence analysis: 1) the data matrix should be large enough that it is essentially uninterpretable via simple descriptive analysis; 2) variables must be "homogeneous" so that statistical row and column distances are interpretable; and 3) the data matrix should be "amorphous, a priori," meaning that the technique is most usefully used in situations where structural relationships are unknown or poorly understood.

7. That is, at or close to zero in both dimensions in figure 4.2.

8. This finding is consistent with high Inequity Index scores in the two higher violence rate regions.

9. In 1986, some 75 percent of homicide victims were male, as were 88 percent of those arrested for homicide (U.S. Department of Justice 1988).

5

Capital Punishment, Race, and Gender

The federal death penalty is almost exclusively sought against minorities, found a DPIC report prepared for the Subcommittee on Civil and Constitutional Rights. *All* those prosecuted by the Clinton administration have been African-Americans. Coverage included: *New York Times, USA Today, Washington Post, Wall Street Journal, AP, UPI and Reuters.*—Excerpt from the World Wide Web home page of the Death Penalty Information Center [DPIC], 9 January, 1996 at www.fenton.com/pub/fenton/death.html.

This chapter is more firmly rooted than the rest of this book in the stream of work relevant to the equity perspective within the geography of criminal justice, including the work of Harries (1974), Harries and Lura (1974), Richardson and Harries (1978), Harries and Brunn (1978), and Blacksell et al. (1986). In the research presented here, we seek to supplement the already extensive literature on race and capital punishment and to add to a little-explored segment of the capital punishment issue—the execution of women. Our concern for equity derives from the fact that fairness is a quality that judicial systems all too often lack, and the apparent inequalities are often based on racial or ethnic discrimination.[1]

The underlying paradigm is simple: equal punishment for equal crime, regardless of race or gender. In the context of capital punishment, the proviso that penalties should be commensurate, or proportional, to crimes, is also germane, given that trivial behaviors, such as cursing one's parents, were once capital offenses. We focus on race and gender given the general social pattern of pervasive discrimination against minority racial groups and women.

Capital Punishment and Race

Execution data since 1900 show that the proportion of African-Americans executed for murder in the South declined from about 80 percent in the first decade of the century to some 40 percent in the 1960s and later, a trend attributed to a combination of migration patterns, changes in legal procedure, and changes in attitudes toward punishment (Schneider and Smykla 1991). While the trend has been for a relative decline in the involvement of African-Americans in executions, recent evidence shows that a pernicious pattern of discrimination remains in the prosecution process in capital cases.

For example, Paternoster (1991) has shown that in South Carolina, capital punishment was more likely to be sought by prosecutors in cases with white victims, compared to African-American. A wealth of comparable evidence pointing to higher execution rates for black offender/white victim incidents, compared to black offender-other race victims, has also been amassed for several other states, including Florida, Kentucky, Georgia, Ohio, and Texas.[2] The effect of the victim's race in South Carolina also varied according to whether the crime occurred in a rural or urban context. Interpretation of this evidence suggests in part that the mostly white-administered justice system tends to place a lower value on black lives than on white, in comparable circumstances. This is consistent with the relationship between perceived crime seriousness and socioeconomic status (SES)—at lower SES levels more violent behavior is regarded as less serious than at higher (Harries 1988; Wolfgang et al. 1985).

Execution, Race, and Execution Eras

The upper left panel of figure 5.1 shows the United States race-specific execution rates of African-Americans and whites since 1790, when the first census enabled the calculation of this measure.[3] This provides a template against which to compare the experiences of individual states. In combination with figures 5.2, 5.3, 5.4, and 5.5, execution rates can be compared in terms of time, space, and race. The five states selected for inclusion in figure 5.1 were those with the largest number of executions: California, Georgia, New York, Pennsylvania, and Virginia.[4]

Detailed analysis of each profile is beyond the scope of this chapter. However, the charts show that rates for whites tended to be consistently low, particularly after about 1800. In contrast, rates for African-Americans were erratic but on average several times higher than those for whites. While black rates were much more erratic than white, in

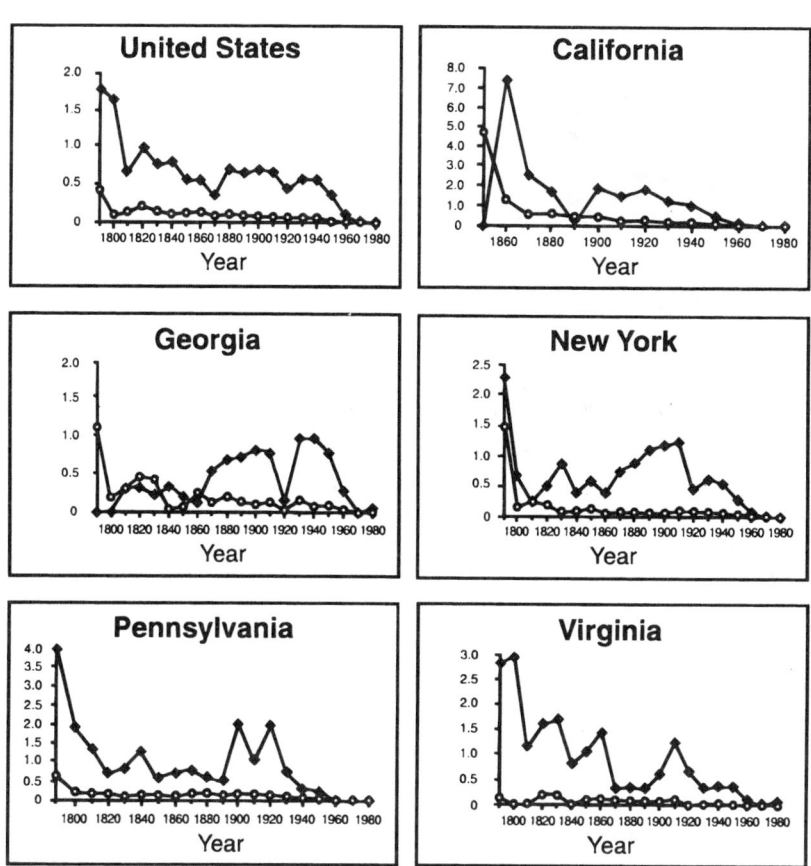

Figure 5.1. Race adjusted execution rates per 10,000, U.S. and selected states. Year scales (horizontal axis) are standardized with the exception of California. Rate scales (vertical axis) vary. *Data sources for Figures 5.1–5.20*: Epsy and Smykla 1987 (executions); ICPSR and U.S. Bureau of the Census (demographic data).

several cases they peaked early, around 1800, and then again around 1900. Differences between states, even southern states, are quite striking; Georgia saw its highest rates of African-American execution relatively recently while Virginia's peaks occurred mostly before 1860, a phenomenon probably associated partly with the apparent penchant, in Virginia, for the execution of escaped slaves and partly with sheer data inadequacy.

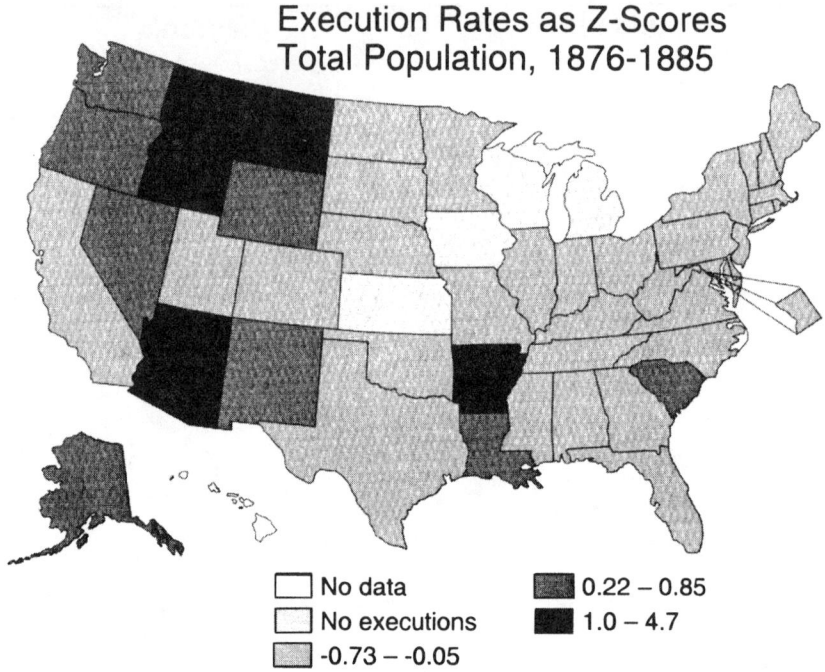

Figure 5.2. Execution rates as Z-scores, total population, 1876–1885.

Figures 5.2 through 5.5 put African-American and total execution rates in a geographic context in two decades, 1876–85 and 1926–35, the former representative of the *growth* era, the latter straddling the *stability* and *peak* periods (see also chapter 2, figures 2.2–2.4). The maps for the earlier decade are based on 1880 census data; the later maps use a 1930 base. Rates in all four maps are expressed in standard deviation units, with a mean of 0.0 and a standard deviation of 1.0. Seen in the context of figures 2.2–2.4, figures 5.2–5.5 are somewhat surprising in their western rather than southern or eastern emphasis. Most striking, perhaps, is the western focus of the African-American execution rate maps for both decades. While explanation is necessarily speculative, it should be noted that the states with exceptionally high rates were sparsely populated; a few executions of members of minority groups would produce extremely high population-specific rates.

This observation begs the question of why such a tiny population group would be subject to executions in the first place, and one is reduced to the surmise that racial minorities in the West were conspicuous and hence more likely to be the objects of discrimination and

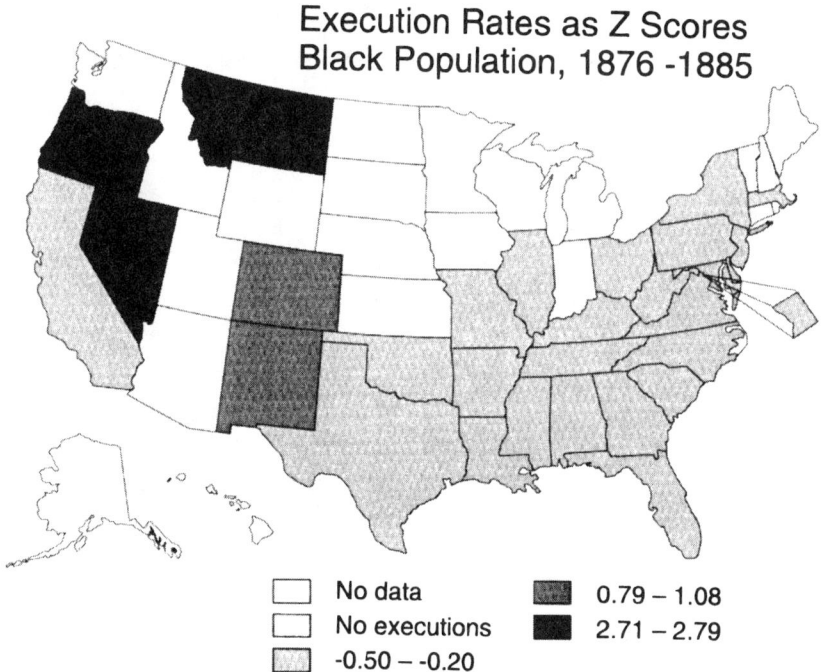

Figure 5.3. Execution rates as Z-scores, African-American population, 1876–1885.

perhaps persecution. This finding of higher western rates is consistent with Bohm (1991b) quoted in chapter 1 to the effect that Gallup polls show that westerners have been among population groups that have supported the death penalty.

Figures 5.6 and 5.7 put African-American executions in the broader context of the percentage distribution of that population, by counties (figure 5.6) and the county-based geography of all executions of African-Americans, excluding lynchings, which would add substantially to the numbers although it might not much affect the geographic distribution. As we would expect, the geography of African-American executions is a reflection of the underlying population distribution. However, these maps mask the disproportionality of the application of capital punishment to the African-American population. Ideally, perhaps we would have a map for each decade to represent that population-based imbalance.

Evidence from the relatively recent past is that young African-Americans, in particular, have been consistently overrepresented in

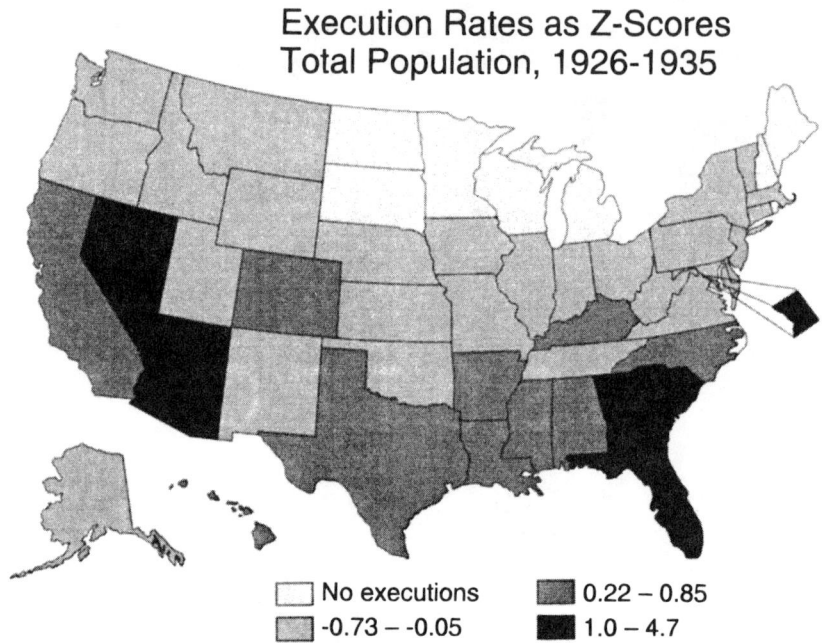

Figure 5.4. Execution rates as Z-scores, total population, 1926–1935.

homicide and other violence rates, as violence has become "juvenilized" (Thomas 1995; Harries 1990; Rose and McClain 1990). This disproportionate involvement of African-Americans in capital crimes has found expression, too, in a complementary literature dedicated specifically to examination of the excessive execution rates of African-Americans (Kleck 1981; Gross and Mauro 1984; Keil and Vito 1989). For example, 52 percent of all executions in the period 1930–1987 were of African-Americans, with 82 percent in the two states in the *very high rate* violence region: Georgia and Alabama (see chapter 4). Yet in Alabama, the percentage of the total population that was black did not exceed 36 in the period 1930–87 (U.S. Bureau of the Census 1983); in Georgia it was never higher than 37 percent, also in 1930 (U.S. Bureau of the Census 1975; 1983).

Capital Punishment and Women

As noted, a considerable research literature has addressed the question of excessive application of the death penalty to African-Americans, but relatively little has been said about the relationship between gender

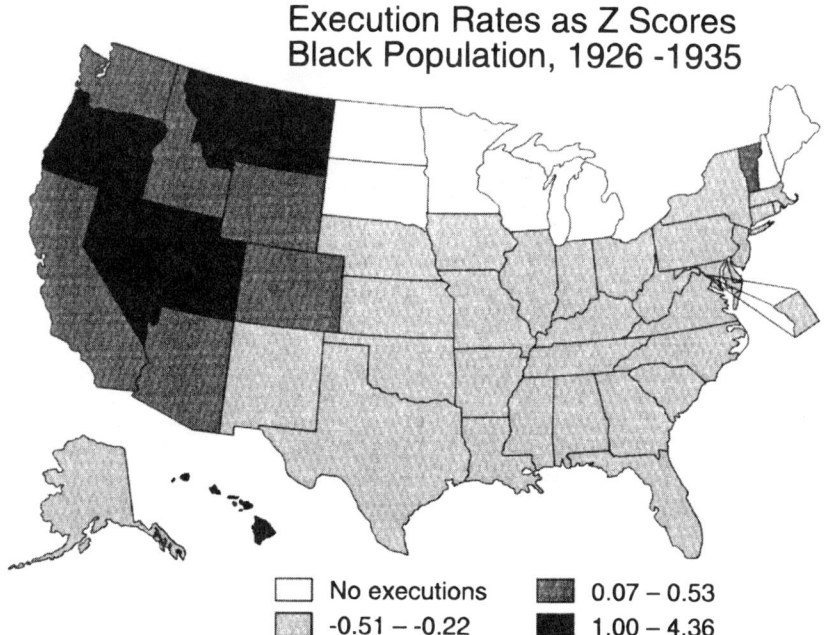

Figure 5.5. Execution rates as Z-scores, African-American population, 1926–1935.

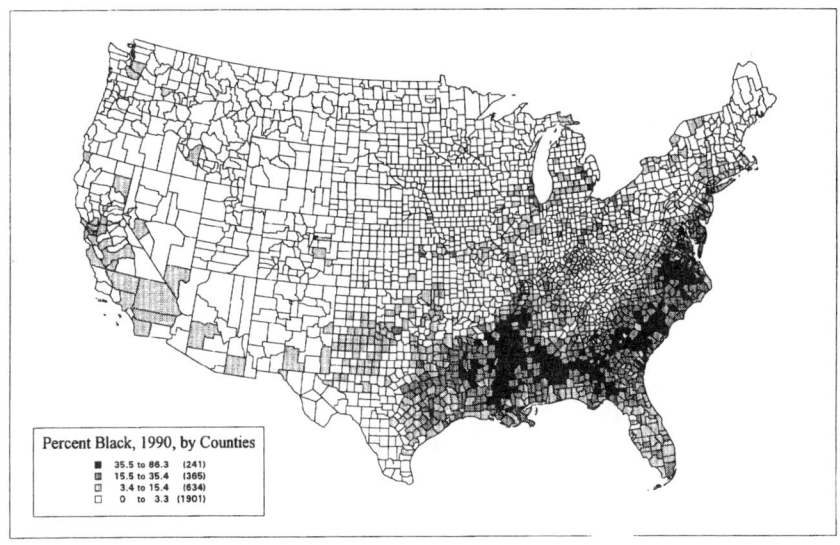

Figure 5.6. Distribution of African-American population, 1990, by counties.

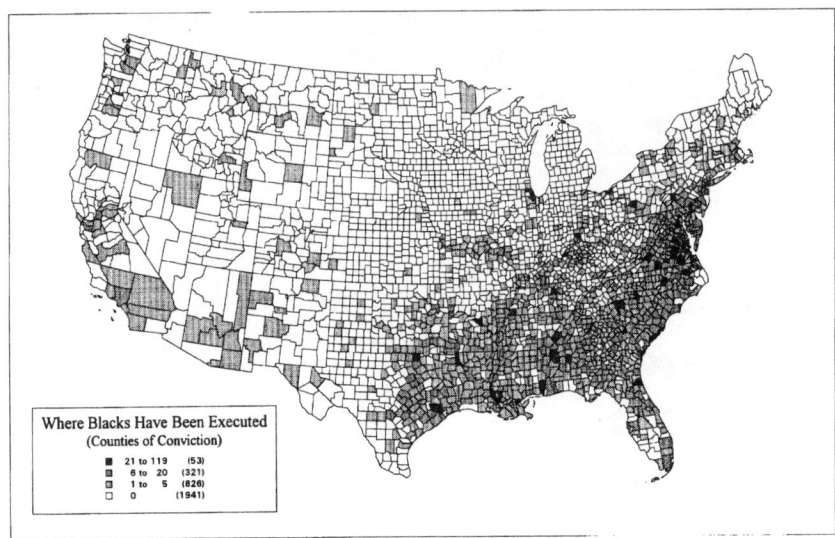

Figure 5.7. Distribution of all executions of African-Americans, by counties.

and execution, perhaps owing to the rather small number of women affected in the course of American history.[5] Even in the contemporary period, with American prisons filled to capacity and the rate of incarceration in the United States higher than in any other more developed country, data showed that at the end of 1990 only 1.4 percent of the prisoners under sentence of death were women (U.S. Department of Justice 1991a; see also Anderson 1983).[6]

Given the upsurge of research on the status of women, it is appropriate to explore how women have fared in the judicial system vis-à-vis capital punishment. More specifically, how have women fared compared to men? A geographic interpretation also seeks to explain place-to-place variations in levels of capital punishment and to put them in a temporal context mediated by both the attributes of the women and men who were executed, and the crimes for which they were convicted.

The temporal framework for the analysis presented here is that adopted by Schneider and Smykla (1991), dividing capital punishment history in the United States into four periods: growth (1608–1879), stability (1880–1929), peak (1930–39), and decline (1940–87). These periods were based on analysis of trends derived from the Espy File and were already illustrated in chapter 2.

The operating hypothesis is that the female and male experiences, *with respect to those people actually executed*, were essentially similar.

Their geographies should resemble each other, their frequencies in each time period should be comparable, and the genders should be comparable with respect to various attributes. Departures from similarity should be explicable in terms of female-male role differences applicable in the relevant time period. For example, the crime of "rape-homicide" is confined to men. Witchcraft was a predominantly female role.

Analysis

Analysis proceeded in four phases. Initially, data for males and females had to be matched. Of the 14,570 executions documented in the first edition of the Espy File covering the period up to 1987, only 357 were of females. This meant that analysis of the female executions was abbreviated in terms of categorical richness compared to males. In order to simulate this sparseness for comparative purposes, a random sample of 357 males was drawn from the total population of males executed, with 1632 (the year of the first female execution) as the first year of eligibility for the male sample.[7] Substantive variables available for analysis were race of offender, age at execution, place of execution, jurisdiction of execution, crime committed, method of execution, date, sex of offender, and occupation of offender.

Some 40 crime categories occur in the complete file, including murder, rape, piracy, desertion, "aiding runaway slaves," forgery, "other," and "not ascertained."[8] Twelve methods of execution were revealed (again, in the complete file): hanging, electrocution, asphyxiation (gas chamber), shooting, injection, "pressing," breaking on the wheel, burning, hanging in chains, bludgeoning, gibbeting, "other," and "not ascertained." Occupations were assigned to more than 700 categories, ranging from buffalo hunter to domestic servant, tugboat fireman, and voodoo doctor.

Regional Distribution

In the second phase, maps were constructed to illustrate the distribution of executions of females and of the male sample, by period. The maps reveal that females were overrepresented in the earliest or growth period (1632–1879) compared to males. The like-size random sample of males produced executions in 26 states compared to 29 for females (figures 5.8, 5.9). While regional concentrations in the Northeast and South are to be expected on the basis of underlying population distribution, two states are particularly conspicuous in the growth period: Virginia and Massachusetts. With 83 and 40 executions

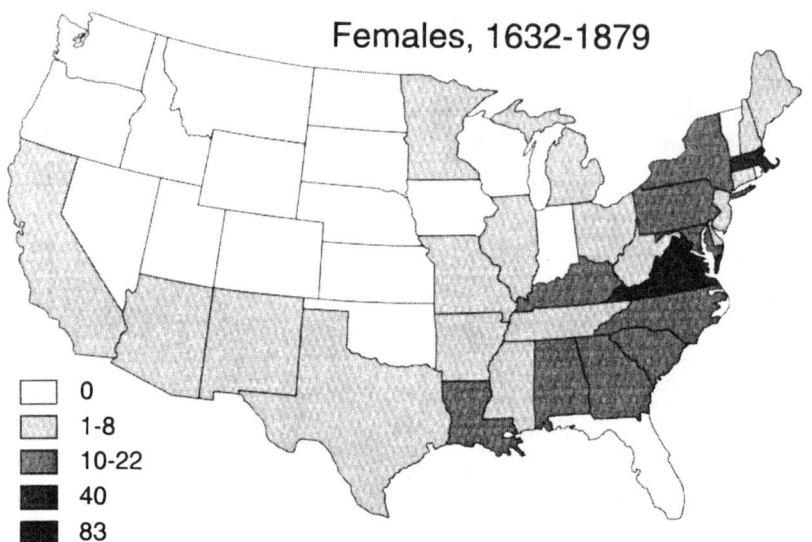

Figure 5.8. Executions of women, 1632–1879.

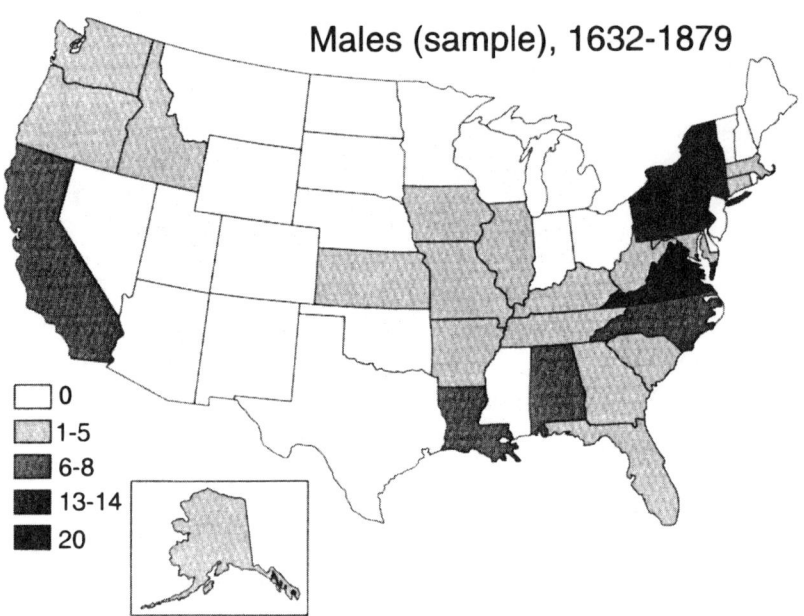

Figure 5.9. Executions of men, 1632–1879. *Note*: In Figs. 5.9, 5.11, 5.13, and 5.15, data for men are based on a random sample of 357. See text for additional explanation.

of women respectively, these states far exceeded the sampled levels of capital punishment for males. The anomaly in Massachusetts was attributable in part to 20 hangings of white women for witchcraft in 1692 in Essex County—the infamous Salem witch trials (Perley 1928; Hansen 1969). In Virginia, the extraordinary total is dominated by executions for murder (64 percent of the executions of females). Eighty-seven percent of the executed Virginia women were slaves.[9]

In the *stability period* (1880–1929) only 32 women were executed (figure 5.10). Geographic scope was limited compared to the male sample (figure 5.11), restricted to the Northeast and South, with the exceptions of Nevada (one event) and California (two). Again, Virginia led in the execution of women, but with a much reduced total of five.

The *peak period* (1930–39) saw only 11 women executed (figure 5.12), compared to the sample of 42 men (figure 5.13). The Northeast and South still dominated, with the addition of Alabama, Illinois, and Ohio, an observation by this time only partially explained by mere population distribution. By now, the impression that women were at less risk of execution than men had been confirmed and continued to be reinforced by examination of the *decline period* (1940–87), when 22 women were put to death, an average of about 2 per year (figure 5.14). During the same period, the random sample of executed men was more than twice that size (figure 5.15).

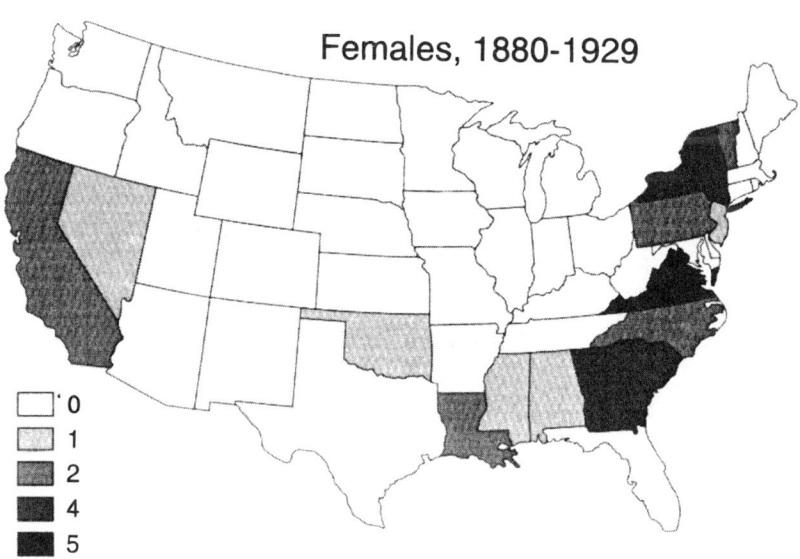

Figure 5.10. Executions of women, 1880–1929.

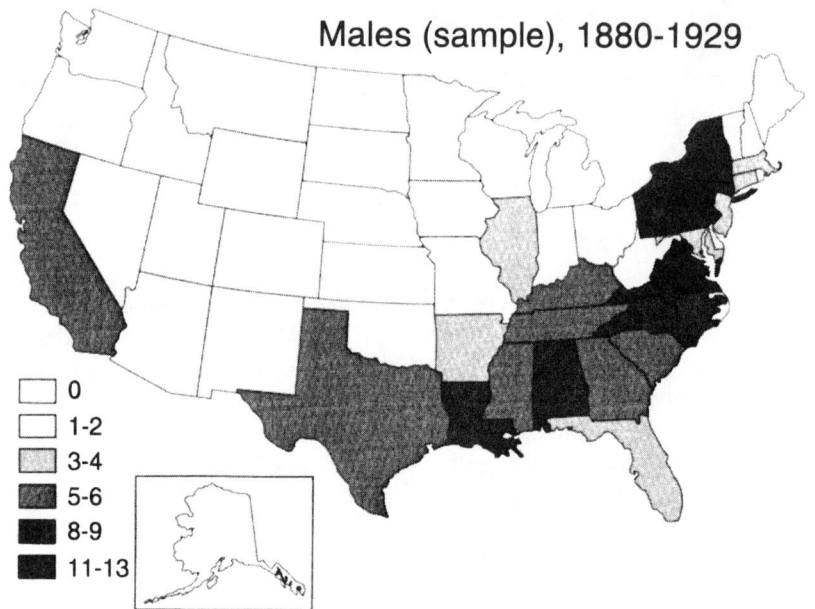

Figure 5.11. Executions of men, 1880–1929.

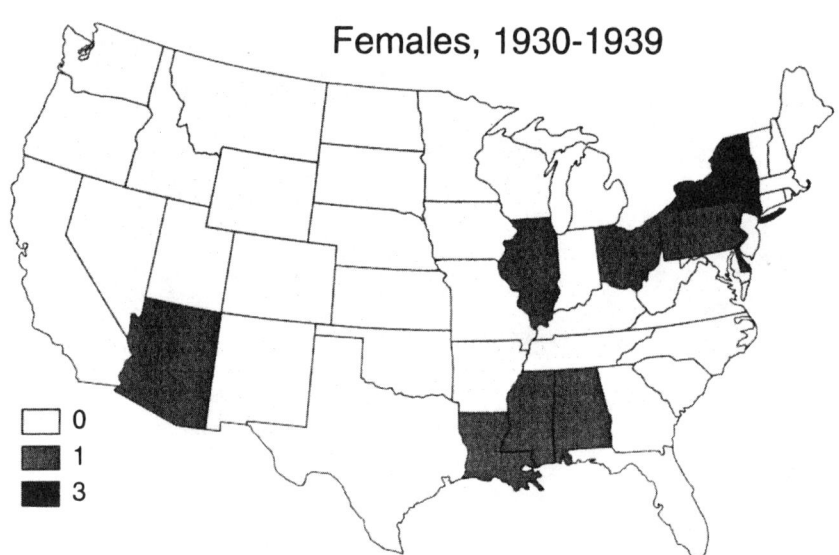

Figure 5.12. Executions of women, 1930–1939.

Capital Punishment, Race, and Gender

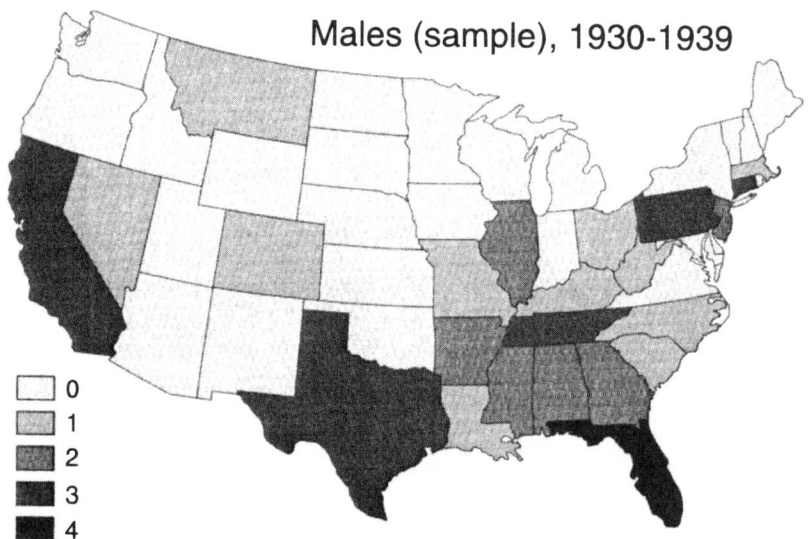

Figure 5.13. Executions of men, 1930–1939.

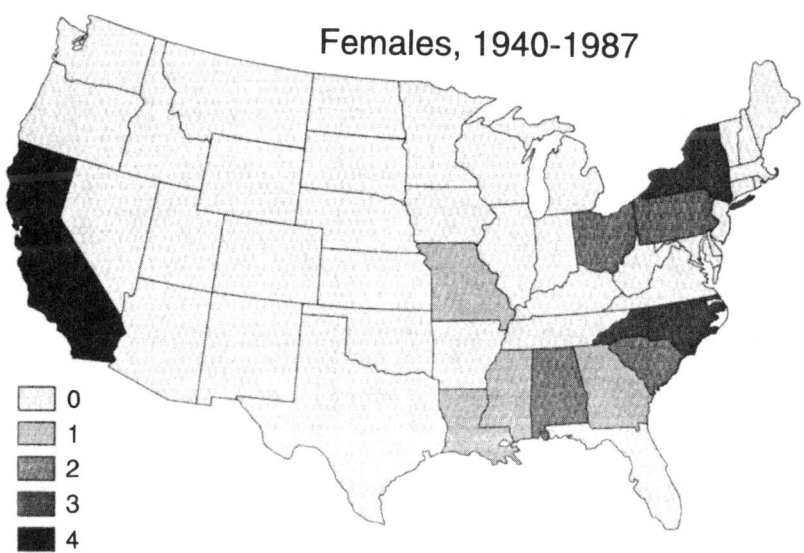

Figure 5.14. Executions of women, 1940–1987.

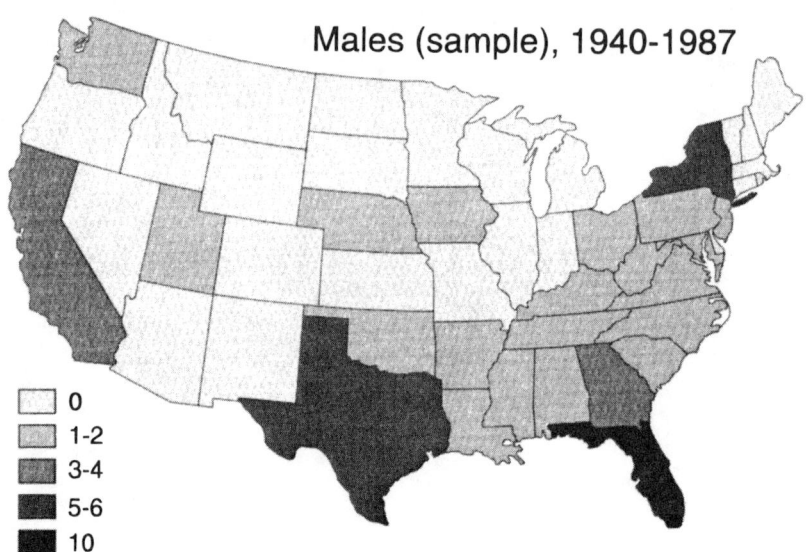

Figure 5.15. Executions of men, 1940–1987.

Attribute Comparisons by Gender

Next, gender comparisons of those executed were made of the demographic characteristics of age, race, and occupation. Crimes for which executions occurred and methods of execution were also matched by gender.

In terms of age and gender, the earlier growth and stability periods were confounded by large "unknown" frequencies, particularly in the growth period, when the age structure was known for only a minority of incidents, with the 20–29 age cohort predominant among that group. A similar situation occurred in the stability period, though with lower frequencies. In the peak and decline periods, too, the 20–29 cohort was dominant. This is consistent with what is known about the general age structure of violent crimes (figure 5.16).

Analysis of race and gender reveals a striking anomaly in the growth period: the preponderance of African-American females. Blacks actually dominate each period, if only slightly, but this too is anomalous given that African-Americans have always constituted a minority of the population (figure 5.17).

The gender structure of occupations of persons executed shows that, again, the "unknown" category, prevalent in earlier years for which records are less complete, somewhat confounds the data. Some categories were expectedly gender-specific, with housewives and servants

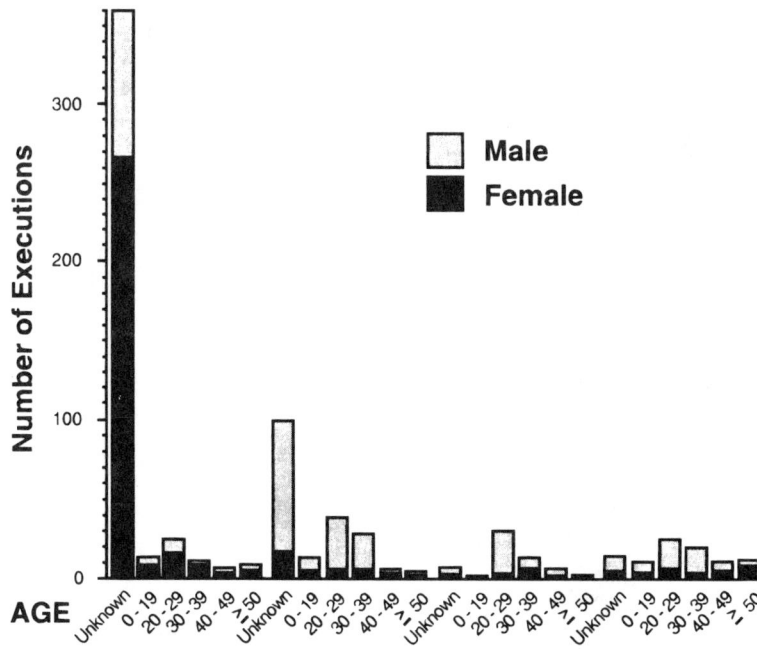

Figure 5.16. Number of executions by gender, age, and period.

only on the female side of the classification. Convicts (already incarcerated) who were adjudged guilty of capital offenses, at least in this sample, were exclusively male. The dominance of the slave category by women is the product of the extraordinary number of executions of slave women in Virginia, referred to above (figure 5.18).

In terms of the crime categories for which women and men were executed, the "unknown" class is relatively insignificant. Women and men contributed about equally to the "murder" category. Rape and rape-murder, as expected, were the sole province of the male sample, which also clearly dominated robbery-murder. Crimes for which only women were executed (according to these data) were: witchcraft, arson, poisoning, and attempted murder. However, it should be noted that this female exclusivity is in part a product of the intentional sparseness of the *male* sample (figure 5.19).

Most women (86 percent) and men (64 percent of the male sample) executed in America have been hanged. Electrocution began in 1890 (during the stability period), and gradually accounted for a larger proportion of all executions, including those of women. (See also chapter 2 for more detail on the origin and diffusion of methods.) The year 1916

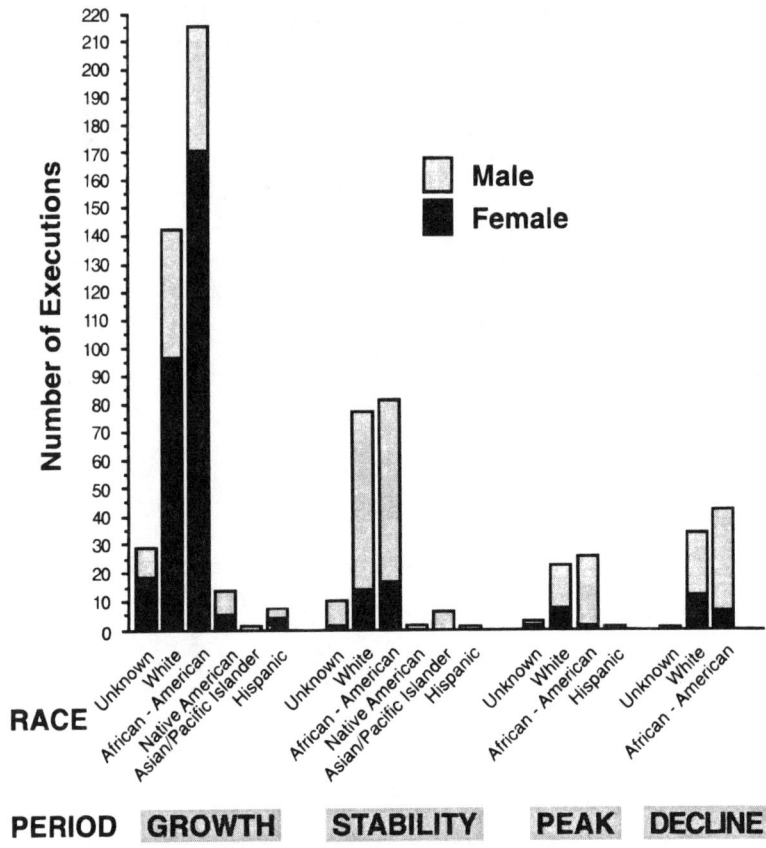

Figure 5.17. Number of executions by gender, race, and period.

was the first in which electrocutions exceeded hangings. Later, other innovative methods emerged.[10] Burning was a punishment meted out almost exclusively to slaves.[11] While no men in the sample data were burned, the complete file shows that 49 men and 15 women were known to have been executed by this method in various states between 1739 and 1825. Only one woman recorded in the first edition of the Espy File died by lethal injection: 52-year-old nurse Velma Barfield, executed for murder in North Carolina on 2 November 1984 (figure 5.20).

Comparative Severity Weighting by Gender

As the next step, a simple crime severity weighting system was applied to a classification of capital crimes in order to assess the question of

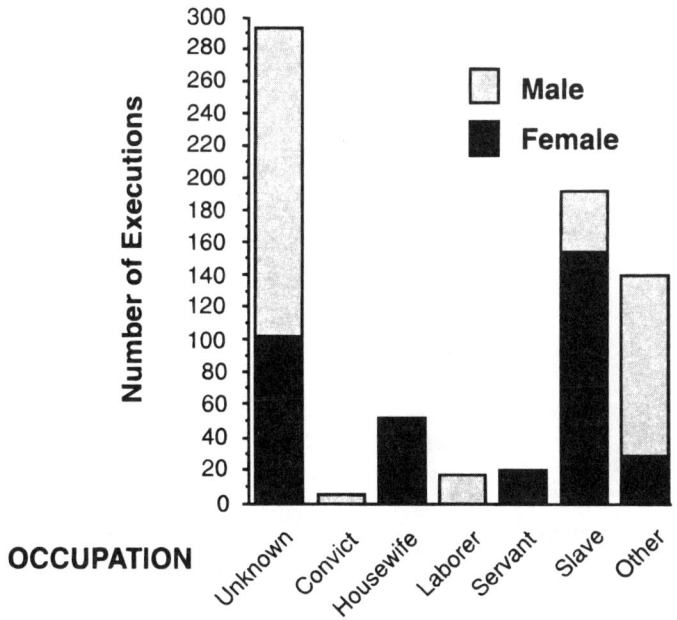

Figure 5.18. Number of executions by gender and occupation.

whether capital punishment was more likely to be applied to women for nonmurder capital offenses, as compared to direct killing roles, by time period. Initially, crimes were dichotomized into (a) those directly resulting in the death of a victim and (b) others.[12] The "direct" crimes were murder, robbery-murder, rape-murder, murder-rape-robbery, murder-burglary, and kidnap-murder. These offenses were assigned a weight of 2. Others were weighted 1. Thus, a female score much lower than male would indicate an emphasis on the execution of women for nonlethal capital offenses such as robbery or forgery. The overall analysis, however, based on 339 females and 349 males, indicated quite similar mean weights (table 5.1). When weights were broken down by period and gender, means were again broadly similar, and differences in means were relatively small and inconclusive (table 5.2). This weighting analysis indicates that, in general, the experience of women and men has been comparable with respect to the types of crimes for which they have been executed. However, it is doubtful that a simple weighting system is capable of capturing all the nuances of this qualitative variation, and there is certainly room for other interpretations.

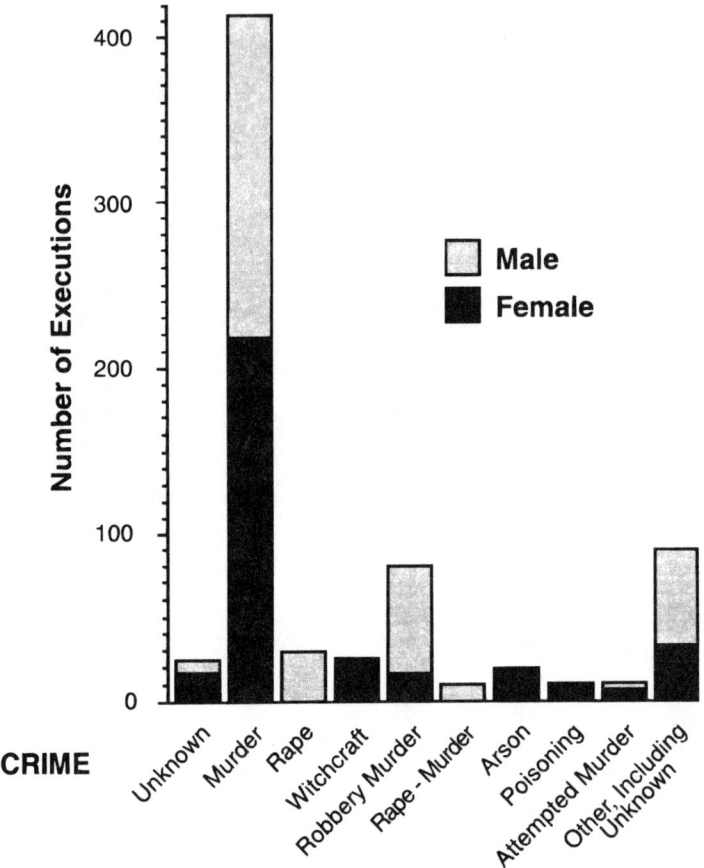

Figure 5.19. Number of executions by gender and crime.

Conclusion

In 1990, most prisoners under sentence of death were white, (54 percent), and some 37 percent were African-American, an astonishing total because blacks make up only 12 percent of the population, but a reflection of the disproportionate involvement of young African-American men in crimes of violence. In 1993, for example, 56.7 percent of all arrests of people over 18 for homicide were of blacks, compared to 41.6 percent white (Maguire and Pastore 1995, table 4.11). Women made up a little more than 1 percent of the total death row population, although this may change since evidence shows not only the involvement of more juveniles in serious, violent crimes but also the involvement of more *female* juveniles. Arrests of female juve-

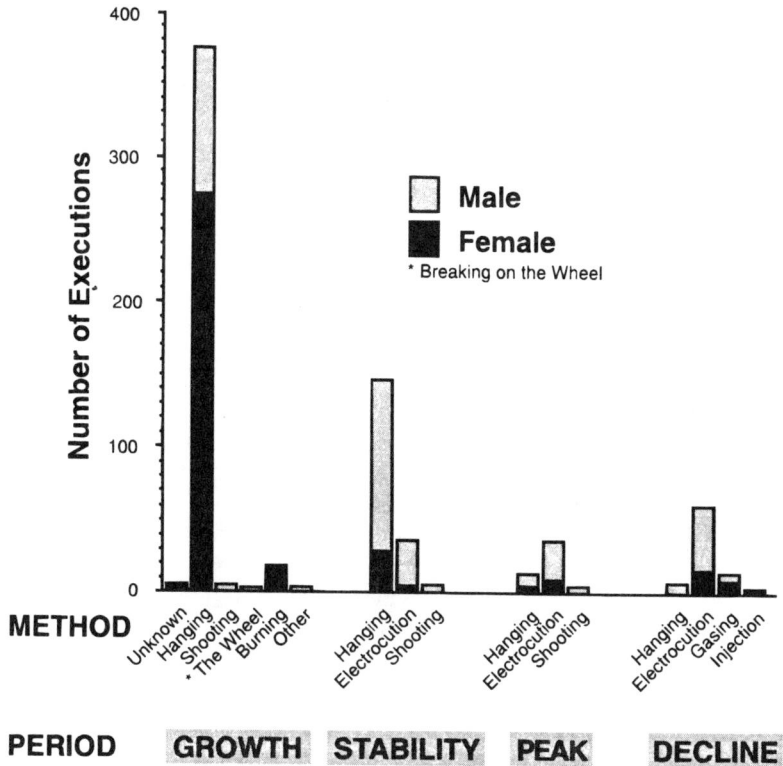

Figure 5.20. Number of executions by gender, method of execution, and period.

Table 5.1. Crime weights by gender.[a]

Gender	Female	Male
N[b]	339	349
Mean weight	1.71	1.79

Source: Calculations by author.
[a]See text for explanation of weights.
[b]Original Ns were 357 for both males and females. Eight male crimes and 18 female crimes were unknown and were removed from the analysis.

Table 5.2. Crime weights by period and gender.

Period	Growth		Stability		Peak		Decline	
Gender	Female	Male	Female	Male	Female	Male	Female	Male
N	276	106	30	144	11	42	22	57
Mean Weight	1.67	1.57	1.93	1.92	1.82	1.86	1.86	1.79

Source: Calculations by author.
See text for explanation of weights.

niles for murder increased almost 18 percent between 1992 and 1993 (Maguire and Pastore 1995, table 4.10).

Over the longer period 1973–1990, the principal death row percentages were similar—56 percent white, 43 percent black (U.S. Department of Justice 1992). This longer series of Department of Justice data relating to death row prisoners reveals a striking discontinuity in the "most serious offenses" for which death row prisoners were incarcerated (table 5.3). African-American defendants were considerably more likely to be imprisoned for crimes other than murder, compared to white defendants. If all the nonmurder crimes are calculated as a percentage of the death row total for the two racial groups (right-hand column in table 5.3), we find that less than 1 percent of whites were on death row for nonmurder, while the comparable figure for blacks was almost 4 percent, with forcible or attempted rape the largest single category.

The disproportionate involvement of blacks in capital punishment is not inappropriate on its face given the high level of involvement of African-Americans in homicide. However, substantial evidence suggests that bias is indeed present, independent of this fact. A recent study

Table 5.3. Most serious offense for which imprisoned: Whites and African-Americans, 1973–1990.

Race	Most serious offense for which imprisoned									
	Murder	Kidnapping or abduction	Forcible or attempted rape	Robbery	Aggravated assault	Hit & run driver with bodily injury	Burglary	Arson	Stolen property	Total
White	2,609	11	11	0	1	1	0	1	0	2,634
Black	1,914	22	45	2	3	0	3	0	2	1,991
Other	63	1	0	0	0	0	0	0	0	64
Total	4,586	34	0	2	4	1	3	1	2	4,689

Data Source: U.S. Department of Justice 1992.

of capital sentencing in the federal judicial system noted that "racial minorities are being prosecuted under federal death penalty law far beyond their proportion in the general population or the population of [federal] criminal offenders." Prosecutions related to the Anti-Drug Abuse Act of 1988 showed that 89 percent of the capital prosecutions were of African-Americans or Mexican-Americans. Furthermore,

> three-quarters of those convicted of participating in a drug enterprise under the general provisions of § 848 have been white and only about 24 percent of the defendants have been black. However, of those chosen for the death penalty prosecutions under this section, just the opposite is true: 78 percent of the defendants have been black and only 11 percent of the defendants have been white ... the almost exclusive selection of minority defendants for the death penalty, and the sharp contrast between capital and noncapital prosecutions under § 848, indicate a degree of racial bias in the imposition of the federal death penalty that exceeds even pre-*Furman* patterns. (Committee on the Judiciary 1994, 1–2. For a detailed comprehensive analysis of the discrimination issue, see: Gross and Mauro 1989.)

Women executed in the course of American history were more likely to be associated with the growth period (1608–1879),[13] to have been African-American, executed for murder,[14] older (or of unknown age), and to have been slaves, in professional occupations, servants, or housewives. Executed men were proportionately more likely to be executed in the three more recent periods, to be younger, executed for a broader array of murder crimes,[15] of "other" ethnicity, and to be of indeterminate or "other" occupation. In terms of method of execution, women were more likely than men to be hanged, although this was merely an expression of the method prevalent in the growth period, when relatively large numbers of women were executed.

The criminal justice literature has focused considerable attention on racial disparities in sentencing and anomalies in other aspects of law and its enforcement. Concern has been expressed, for example, about the status of the mentally handicapped with respect to capital punishment, and the finding that juries are less likely to convict in capital cases has introduced further ambivalence into the capital punishment issue (Chan 1990; Freedman 1990).

The lack of attention, historically, to the issue of gender and capital punishment may be due to the relatively small number of women executed in the course of American history, less than about 2.5 percent of all executions. This observation is attributable to the persistently low level of involvement of women in crimes of violence, a condition that continues in force today, but that seems to be changing, particularly with respect to juvenile female offenders. Nevertheless, the death of 357 women is hardly trivial.

A factor that also deserves mention with respect to the execution of women is that American culture may be less willing to accept the execution of females compared to males, and this condition may vary on a regional basis. While it is well established that women are less involved in capital offenses than are men, the gender disparity in capital punishment appears to be extreme. In the period 1976–1993, the percentage of female offenders committing murder and nonnegligent manslaughter was 8.1 for 14–17-year-olds, 10.5 for 18–24-year-olds, and 15.4 for those 25 years and older, yet only about 1 percent of the occupants of death rows were female, and only one of the 313 executions between the resumption of capital punishment in 1977 and the end of 1995 was of a woman (Maguire and Pastore 1995, table 3.120). However, women commit fewer of the kinds of crimes that generally attract death sentences; even taking this into account, disparity remains between men and women.[16]

A relatively new dimension specifically affecting women (and further confounding comparisons between men and women on death rows) is what has come to be called the "battered spouse syndrome," apparently originating in the case of Bernadette Peters, who shot and killed her husband in New York in 1978 (Anderson 1983). State laws increasingly allow this defense to women who kill partners and who are able to bring to bear evidence to the effect that they were victims of a pattern of abuse, one response to which was reciprocal violence in self-defense. The net result of the application of such laws should be to depress the female population of death rows. However, trends toward social and economic equity in other realms and the increased numbers of juvenile female violent offenders may tend to have a countervailing effect.

Notes

1. See for example, the case of the so-called "Birmingham Six" released from prison in England in March 1991. These Irishmen had been convicted 16 years previously for bombing a public house in Birmingham. In retrial, it emerged that erroneous forensic analysis, forced confessions, and other miscarriages had surrounded the original police investigation. Even the retrial process itself was obstructed for years by a recalcitrant high court judge.

2. For more comprehensive discussion, see Keil and Vito 1991, Gross and Mauro 1989, and the conclusion of this chapter.

3. This differs from figure 2.1, which represented raw frequencies, and figure 2.10 (dashed line), a crude rate for the total population.

4. Note that the rate (vertical) scales on each part of figure 5.1 are identical, but the time (horizontal) scales differ.

5. For example, the authoritative compilation of readings edited by Bedau and Pierce (1976) has no chapter dealing explicitly with the issue of gender; neither does the more recent review edited by Bohm (1991b).

6. This percentage is based on a total of 2,250, of whom 1,295 were white males, 893 black males, and 37 males of other races. The 1.1 percent that women represent was made up of 15 whites and 10 blacks.

7. In order to assess the categorical stability of male samples, several samples of 357 males were drawn and reviewed. Their categorical structures were quite similar. In order to avoid unnecessarily limiting the scope of description and comparison by invariably confining analysis of male executions to the sample of 357, the whole file is drawn from as the context warrants.

8. Given that female executions totaled 357 and a sample of 357 males was drawn, only a selection of crimes, methods of execution, and occupations were present in the data dealt with here.

9. The Virginia total may seem relatively large for artifactual reasons. A project to research such data more intensively ran out of resources before all relevant states could be covered.

10. Analysis of the complete file showed that in 1916 there were 58 electrocutions and 48 hangings. By 1939, hanging was all but extinct (14 hangings, 118 electrocutions). The first year in the twentieth century without a hanging was 1964. Gas was first used in 1924, lethal injection in 1982.

11. Only one nonslave was recorded in the Espy File as having been burned, a "housewife."

12. "Unknowns" were removed from further consideration.

13. Thirty-one percent of all male executions took place in the growth period, compared to 82 percent of all executions of women. Comparable percentages for the other periods were: stability—male 41, female 9; peak—12, 3; decline—16, 6.

14. See tables 5.1 and 5.2 and figure 5.19 for a more detailed appraisal of the crimes for which women and men were executed.

15. Apart from "ordinary" murder, robbery-murder was dominated by males. See figure 5.19.

16. A case that attracted considerable attention in early 1996 was the commutation of the death sentence of Guinevere Garcia by Illinois Governor Jim Edgar. According to Felten (1996), Garcia was "a prime candidate for death row . . . her crime was a paradigm of capital murder. Mr. Edgar's show of mercy, it would seem, had less to do with her crime than with her gender."

6

Capital Punishment and the Deterrence of Violent Crime in Comparable Counties

The deterrence argument for capital punishment claims that the existence of the death penalty and the use of that penalty will deter violent crime within the political jurisdiction in which the law exists and is applied. If that is true, then in two fundamentally similar jurisdictions that differ only in the existence and use of capital punishment, the level of violent crime in the jurisdiction that employs the death penalty should be lower than the level in the jurisdiction that does not.

Past comparative research has suggested that this is not the case. However, most of the research on deterrence has relied on large units of analysis, seldom smaller than states or nations, with the attendant problems of data aggregation and comparability of units. The larger the jurisdictions, the more heterogeneous they become and the less sure we can be of controlling for extraneous factors or guaranteeing true comparability between the entities examined.

To counteract these problems, the research reported in this chapter employs socioeconomic and capital punishment variables for 1,725 counties in the United States and for a smaller select sample of 293 matched pairs of counties. The use of counties not only significantly expands the sample size but also addresses the problem of data aggregation by dealing with more compact and homogenous units. At the same time, employing 293 pairs of contiguous counties confronts the issue of comparability by directly contrasting political entities that are inherently similar in terms of their human and physical geographies, their regional settings, and their broad developmental characteristics.

Differences between the pairs of matched counties on those economic and sociodemographic characteristics that have proven significant correlates of serious violent crime are then tested as predictors of differences in the violent crime rate between the counties. Further, each contiguous pair consists of counties in two different states, so the use of capital punishment will vary across each pair. This variation, then, is also tested as a predictor of the difference in the level of violent crime between the two adjacent counties. By studying matched counties in which the existence of capital punishment statutes or the level of use of those statutes varies, we should have improved the conditions to test deterrence theory in comparative settings. Based upon the weight of the prior research, we posit that *neither the existence of a provision for capital punishment at the state level, the use of the provision as demonstrated by the number of inmates sentenced to death, nor the enactment of that provision as demonstrated by the actual number of executions in the state since 1976, has the effect of deterring violent crime at the county level.*

Review of the Question

The Debate Over the Deterrent Effect of Capital Punishment

There is an ongoing debate over the utility of the death penalty in deterring violent crime. Two different research traditions offer contradictory answers to the question of the efficacy of deterrence. Good general reviews of the material are found in a number of studies, most recently Peterson and Bailey (1991) and Decker and Kohfeld (1990). What follows is a relatively brief review of the major points of the traditions that most directly apply to this research.

The fundamental question is whether capital punishment serves to deter violent crime. A tradition of structural comparisons has evolved out of research largely initiated by Thorsten Sellin in 1959, although others had reached similar conclusions even earlier (Sutherland 1925; Vold 1932). The studies of this type are variations on a theme, using international, national, regional, or state data to compare jurisdictions that have capital punishment with those that do not or, in some cases, jurisdictions before and after the abolition of capital punishment. Virtually no comparative study demonstrates deterrent effects from capital punishment (Archer, Gartner, and Beittel 1983; Bailey 1977, 1982, 1991; Black and Orsagh 1978; Bowers and Pierce 1980b; Decker and Kohfeld 1990; Forst 1977; Grogger 1990; Lempert 1983; McFarland 1983; Passell and Taylor 1977; Peterson and Bailey 1991; Sellin 1959; Zimring and Hawkins 1986). This is true whether the research measures de jure or de facto capital punishment, the level of use of the penalty, uses cross-state or cross-national material, or examines abolition or reinstatement of the penalty. It also holds true despite the time period examined. The range of data, methodology, technique, and approach that have produced findings of no deterrent effect of capital punishment, then, are substantial. Moreover, a series of more focused research has examined the effect that capital punishment has on prison killings (Buffum 1973), police killings (Bailey 1982), or felony murders (Peterson and Bailey 1991) and has also found no deterrent effect on these more specific behaviors.

On the other hand, a stream of longitudinal studies, initiated by Isaac Ehrlich in 1975, used econometric methods and data at the national level to test the level of violent crime against changes in execution patterns. Some researchers in this latter approach, in contrast to the comparative studies, claim to have demonstrated a deterrent effect (Chressanthis 1989; Cloninger 1977; Layson 1985; Yunker 1982; and to some degree Cover and Thistle 1988). These claims reach as high as the saving of 156 murder victims for each execution (Yunker 1982).

This approach, particularly the work of Ehrlich, has been severely criticized. These criticisms relate primarily to the fact that the apparent deterrent effects are dependent upon the time period used, the specification of the variables, the quality of the data used and, in Ehrlich's work, the transformations made in the data (Bowers 1988; Bowers and Pierce 1975; Fox and Radelet 1987; McGahey 1980; Passell and Taylor 1977; see also Hoenack and Weiler 1980). While subsequent researchers specifically addressed these critiques in their work (Layson 1985), even those who have attempted some of the more sophisticated corrections find mixed support for the deterrence argument in economic models and conclude that the findings of a "deterrent effect of capital punishment are sensitive to the functional form of the regression [employed] and the empirical definitions of the expected probabilities of punishment" (Cover and Thistle 1988, 617).

In addition, and in direct opposition to the fundamental assumptions of the deterrence argument, other researchers have suggested a "brutalization" effect of capital punishment (Bowers and Pierce 1980b). Tests of this concept, which examine data ranging from the short-term effects of publicized homicides to the long-term effects of executions nationally, find everything from possible support of this idea (Bailey 1991) through no support for deterrence or brutalization (McFarland 1983; Peterson and Bailey 1991) to evidence of a short-term deterrent effect followed by a mid-term brutalization effect, producing, in the long run, a balance (Phillips 1980; Stack 1987).

Both positions on deterrence continue to have adherents and detractors. Criminologists who have considered the pros and cons in a comparative analysis of the two positions (Baldus and Cole 1975; Barnett 1981; Forst 1983; Gibbs 1977; Wolfgang 1978) generally agree that the dispute remains unresolved in the professional literature, much as it does in society, although others clearly find the weight of the evidence is against deterrence (Bowers 1988). We conclude that the bulk of the evidence appears to dictate rejection the notion of a deterrent effect of capital punishment, despite some evidence to the contrary.

The comparative studies that constitute the bulk of this research have been contaminated to some extent by the large size of the units studied and the resulting compound difficulties with aggregation. The samples employed and the units of analysis have varied from cross-cultural comparisons of nation-states (Rahiv 1983), through the 50 United States (Bailey 1982), selected states (Decker and Kohfeld 1991), or single states (Grogger 1990), down to selected local jurisdictions (Bailey 1984b). These studies, then, suffer from questions regarding the comparability of the jurisdictions examined and the lack of control over certain variables.

The Problem of Comparability and Counties as Units of Analysis

Baldus and Cole (1977) note that the problem of holding constant other factors besides capital punishment that might influence homicide is shared by the tradition evolving from Sellin and that derived from Ehrlich. They observe that Sellin's matching method, which underlies much of the comparative research, is "simply a different technique for taking [these factors into] account" (Baldus and Cole 1975, 177). As Barnett notes (1981), one of the problems with any comparative approach is that it is difficult to find genuinely comparative jurisdictions, particularly when the sample is limited to the 50 states.

The goal is, of course, to find the smallest, least aggregated, or most homogenous units of analysis possible so that there is control "for the effect of other variables by comparing areas which are as similar as possible with respect to those variables, but are different with respect to the variable whose effect is being isolated" (Baldus and Cole 1975, 177).

The research reported on here is based upon counties, in the belief that they most comprehensively meet these demands. Counties are generally smaller and more homogeneous units, avoiding the large-scale aggregation of data inevitable at state or national levels. While counties are less commonly used than Metropolitan Statistical Areas or states, they have been employed as units of analysis by Kowalski and associates in studies of the effect of urban-rural differences on homicide rates (Kowalski and Duffield 1990) and on suicide rates

(Kowalski, Faupel, and Starr 1987). As they point out, one of the significant advantages of using counties is that it "may substantially reduce the hazards associated with aggregation, by bringing the statistics closer to actual social reality" (Kowalski and Duffield 1990, 177–178).

At the same time, our method of matching further controls for effects of season, climate, physical features, and region and assumes a roughly similar general development history for each pair of counties. The use of contiguous counties in two states, one with the death penalty and the other without, also allows for some examination of the hypothesis of displacement. Finally, the use of counties also allows for a much larger sample size than has been possible in any prior research.

Sample and Methodology

Sample

The original full data set consists of 1,725 counties drawn from the *County and City Data Book* for 1988 (U.S. Bureau of the Census 1988). This constitutes all counties in the United States with populations of 20,000 or more. Data on key variables, including race, gender, and age composition, are reported in the *County and City Data Book* only for counties of that size or larger, so the data set includes all counties in the United States for which there was adequate information on the variables employed for analysis (from a total of 3,191 counties). This, of course, produces some bias in the data, unavoidable given the data available. The benefits derived from the larger sample of more homogenous counties (compared to states or nations) seems to justify use of the sample, even taking these problems into account. It is important, however, to keep this in mind when considering the results.

The final sample sought for the research was a specific set of counties in the United States that inherently controlled for a number of fundamental variables. A method to assure comparability on the dimensions of geography, regional context, and historical development, and yet allow variance in state patterns in the use of capital punishment, is to *select all pairs of counties in the United States that share a majority of a contiguous border across a state line*. This is certainly not a common technique, and the procedure for determining such pairs is described below. We must note that a more precise or formal description is given first, but must also acknowledge that the criterion used is somewhat difficult to visualize. We also attempt to offer simple, concrete examples to assist the reader with this visualization (figure 6.1).

Capital Punishment and Deterrence

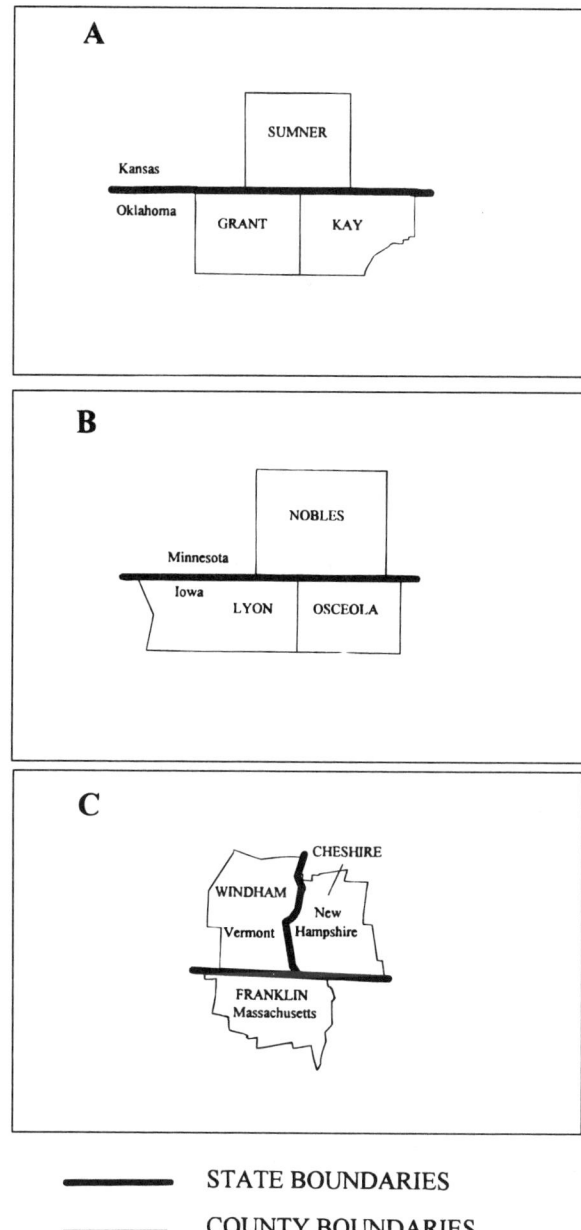

STATE BOUNDARIES

COUNTY BOUNDARIES

Figure 6.1. Examples of contiguous countries. *Source*: authors.

In figure 6.1-A, Sumner County, Kansas, is contiguous to Grant County, Oklahoma, and to Kay County, Oklahoma, since it shares at least 45 percent of its contiguous border with both counties, and both Grant and Kay share at

In 1990, we located every pair of counties in the United States that mutually shares 45 percent or more of their borders across a state line. We originally planned to use counties that shared a majority of their mutual boundaries, that is, 50 percent or more. But in a surprising number of cases, determining precisely this "50 percent" measure proved to be difficult, since one county would share almost exactly that amount with two other counties (as in figure 6.1A). To account for this, we adopted the more forgiving 45 percent figure.

First, we looked at every county that had a border on a state line. If 45 percent or more of that border was shared by a county across that state line, we then asked whether that second county also shared 45 percent of its border with the first county. So, for example, over 45 percent of the southern border of York County, Pennsylvania, *and* 45 percent of the northern border of Baltimore County, Maryland, are shared. In some cases, one county shared one border with two other counties or shared two borders across two states (when on the "corner" of a state, for example). In these cases, a die was rolled to determine which pair of counties would be used in the analysis. As a result, no county was included more than once; see figure 6.1.

This process of matching enabled us to do two things. First, in comparing these counties, we controlled for the features discussed above. The topography, climate, and general ethnic, economic, and social history of any specific portion of northern Mississippi and southern Tennessee, for example, are virtually indistinguishable. The same is true for the topography, climate, and history of northeastern Virginia compared to southwestern Maryland, or the panhandle of Florida compared to southern Alabama. Yet some measures of southernness would place Mississippi, Tennessee, and Virginia together, while separating

---

least 45 percent of their borders with Sumner County in return. In this case, a coin toss would have determined whether the matched pair would constitute Sumner and Grant, or Sumner and Kay.

In figure 6.1-B, Nobles County, Minnesota, is contiguous to Osceola County, Iowa, since both share at least 45 percent of their mutual border with the other, but is not contiguous with Lyon County, Iowa, since Lyon does not share that percentage of its border with Nobles.

In figure 6.1-C, Cheshire County, New Hampshire, is adjacent to two counties in two different states. It shares all of its western border with Windham County, Vermont, and some of its southern border with Franklin County, Massachusetts. Only Windham shares over 45 percent of its mutual border with Cheshire, so one matched pair could be Cheshire and Windham. Another possibility is Windham and Franklin, since they also share more than 45 percent of their mutual border with each other and are in different states.

Maryland from Virginia. And cross-state comparisons would find the suburbs of Washington, D.C. in the same classification as villages in the Shenandoah Valley, or Miami, Florida, grouped with Leonia (population 200), Florida. Our sample of contiguous counties addresses this problem by comparing Hardeman County, Tennessee directly with Benton County, Mississippi, Montgomery County, Maryland, with Loudoun County, Virginia, and Holmes County, Florida, with Geneva County, Alabama. Geographic factors that may have had a significant effect on social or historical development (specifically rivers or lakes) are dealt with in the analysis (see the methodology section following).

Second, such matching enables us to identify counties that share these geographic, climatic, and developmental features, yet that exist in jurisdictions that differ (by virtue of being in different states) on the presence of a capital punishment statute (in some cases), or on the number of inmates on death row or the number of persons executed since 1976 in all cases.

Again, an example illustrates the methodology. Cowley County in Kansas shares over 45 percent of its southern border with the northern border of Kay County in Oklahoma. These counties are small enough in size that they are relatively homogenous in the socio-demographic characteristics of their population, yet they are separated by the legal codes of the two states in which they lie. Oklahoma allows for capital punishment; Kansas did not when this project was undertaken. Further, even if two states have provisions for capital punishment, they will vary in the degree to which they sentence their citizens to death and the degree to which they carry out those sentences. Thus, citizens of Holmes County, Florida, are in a state that has executed 27 people since 1979 and holds 315 people on death row, whereas only a few miles away in Geneva County, Alabama, residents are in a state that has executed 9 people since 1983 and holds 115 on death row as of spring, 1992 (NAACP Legal Defense Fund 1992).

Incidentally, the comparison of contiguous counties in two states, only one of which has the death penalty, allows for a limited test of the displacement hypothesis. If the homicide offender is the logical actor required by deterrence theory, then the existence of the death penalty should prompt offenders to change the location of their crime when possible. If this were the case, an offender should choose an abolitionist state in which to commit a felony if it required nothing more than crossing a county line. This should be particularly true in our case, since our crime data include the supposedly more planned offense of robbery. However, our data allow only for a limited consideration of this question. If crime rates are higher in abolitionist states' counties, it could imply either that deterrence works or that displacement is occurring, and we would not be in a position to make even tentative claims regarding displacement. However, if crime rates are not higher in abolitionist states, then the nature of the sample involved would clearly imply that displacement is *not* occurring.

After eliminating duplicated counties, we found 786 such counties, or 393 matched pairs, in the United States. Again, however, not all of these have adequate data for analysis. The final study, then, is based on 293 matched pairs of these counties, comparing 586 counties in all.

Variables from *The County and City Data Book*

The variables included in the analysis have been drawn from the literature on the correlates of violent crime at a variety of geographic scales, ranging from cities to nation-states. A set of 13 key variables that recur repeatedly in the literature on violent crime were selected from the *County and City Data Book* for 1988. These variables were: *population, population per square mile, percent nonwhite, male-female ratio, percentage aged 15 to 24, percentage aged 24 to 34, percentage of female-headed households, infant deaths per 1,000 births, percentage with 12+ years education, percentage below the poverty level, percentage of owner-occupied homes, unemployment rate,* and *per capita income.* In addition, the number of violent crimes was taken from this source and the *county violent crime rate* computed as the dependent variable.

Both methodological considerations and recent work by Bailey and Peterson (1990) support the use of violent crime rates rather than capital murder rates as the dependent variable. Bailey and Peterson used a monthly time-series analysis of executions and execution publicity effects, on rates of Type I (most serious) Uniform Crime Reports (UCR) crimes (with the exception of murder and arson) to test the premise that ". . . capital punishment may affect other crimes . . . that put victims' lives at risk" (Bailey and Peterson 1990, 682). The results indicate an impact of executions on rates of robbery, burglary, and—(most especially)—aggravated assault. Indeed, this research finds stronger deterrent effects for these crimes than have been found for murder.

Methodologically, the availability of the data and the theoretical operation of deterrent effects (if any) in real-world populations both argue for the use of violent crime rates (see Bailey and Peterson [1990] for a discussion of the theorized processes operating). Only the violent crime rate is reported in the *County and City Data Book*, and using murder data for smaller counties would necessitate not only using another data source, but in some cases aggregating data over periods of 5–10 years (or more) to ensure capturing at least one murder in small counties. This, of course, means that accounting for changes in other variables over that span of years becomes a problem. Given all these considerations, the general violent crime rate remains the dependent variable employed.

It is beyond the scope of this chapter to discuss the abundance of research that supports the inclusion of the chosen independent variables. Readers are referred to the works cited below only because they are the most recent or some of the most seminal in the ongoing debate over the importance of these factors and because they contain thorough reviews of the previous literature on the topic.

The centrality of density or urbanization to levels of violence across a geographic scale is well documented (Archer and Gartner 1984; Decker and Kohfeld 1990; Kowalski and Duffield 1990; Krahn, Hartnagel and Gartrell 1986; Land, McCall and Cohen 1990; Sampson 1985), and two variables were coded as potential measures of this: population and population density. We assumed that population density is the most obvious measure, in that it is a crude metric of potential interactions between people, including those that involve criminal violence. However, we remained open to the possibility that the absolute number of people in the geographic area may be the critical factor and left in a measure to allow for this.

Our analysis shares three of the measures employed in the Kowalski and Duffield (1990) county-level homicide study—percentage nonwhite, percentage ages 15–34 (computed from two variables), and percentage below the poverty level. Other measures they used reflected concerns not shared here (predominantly related to rurality or farm economics) or were captured through the use of other measures (e.g., *percentage with 12+ years of education* versus *median years of education*).

The recurrent association of violent crime with measures of race (U.S. Centers for Disease Control 1986; Golden and Messner 1987), age (Block 1986; Cheatwood and Block 1990; Land et al. 1990), and gender (Harries 1990; Messner and Sampson 1991; Reidel, Zahn, and Mock 1985) is captured with figures on percentage nonwhite, the male-to-female ratio, and the percentage of the population aged 15–34 (computed from two variables in the data). The literature on violent crime clearly indicates that the ages from 15 to 34 are those of highest involvement (U.S. Centers for Disease Control 1986; Reidel et al. 1985). Similarly, one of the most consistent correlates of criminal involvement is failure in school, measured by the percentage of the population with 12 years or more of education. (See Hirschi 1969, for theory and research on this, especially pp. 113–130.)

The final six variables are all surrogate measures of economic well-being. All have been used in various studies as economic measures (see Bailey 1984a; Rosenfeld and Messner 1991). Some are quite obvious, specifically the percentage below the poverty level, the unemployment rate, and per capita income (see Loftin and Parker 1985). The remaining three have been shown to be reliable indicators of the real level of economic deprivation in ways that might be hidden by more obvious monetary measures, specifically: infant deaths per 1,000 (Loftin and Hill 1974), percentage of female headed households (Messner and Sampson 1991; Sampson 1987), and percentage of owner-occupied homes (Lander 1954; see also Massey and McKean 1985).

Finally, from *Death Row, USA*, published by the NAACP Legal Defense Fund, each county was coded as to whether it was in a state with or without a death penalty statute, the number of people being held on death row as of spring 1992 in the state in which each county appears, and the number of people executed in each county's state since 1976 (NAACP Legal Defense Fund 1992).

Findings

A first series of multiple regressions was run on the full set of 1,725 counties without inclusion of the capital punishment variables. A second set of equations was then computed with the capital punishment variables included. The purpose was to see what variables appeared to be important without the capital punishment measures in the analysis. Again, these analyses are only preliminary to the central analyses of the data for the matched pairs.

Tests of intercorrelation and examination of a number of preliminary multiple regressions led to the inclusion of 9 of the original 13 independent variables in the final multivariate analyses of the full county sample: population density (DENSITY), males per 100 females (SEXRATIO), percentage of female households (%FEMHEAD), infant deaths per 1,000 births (INFTDETH), percentage below poverty level (%POVERTY), percentage of owner-occupied housing (%OWNHOME), the unemployment rate (UNEMPLOY), per capita income (PERCAPIN), and percentage age 15 to 34 (%15TO34).

Thus, from the original 13 variables, percentage age 15 to 24 and percentage age 25 to 34 were combined into 1 variable, and 3 variables (population, percentage with 12+ years of education, and percentage nonwhite) were dropped. The latter variable, percentage nonwhite, is one of the more common correlates in the literature but was deleted because of its high correlation with the percentage of female households and the fact that when substituted in the multiple regressions for percentage of female households, its effect was less than the factor for which it was substituted. The same is true for the education measure (percentage with 12+ years of education), which was highly correlated with per capita income, yet was not as influential in the multiple regression analysis, and population, which had a similar relationship to the measure of density.

From these nine variables, six enter in the first regression equation, with the rate of violent crime as the dependent or "predicted" variable (see table 6.1). Of these six, three explain 36 percent of the variance in the homicide rate, while the remaining three variables that enter add less than an additional 1 percent. Pragmatically, then, the key variables in predicting the violent crime rate in the larger sample are the percentage of female-headed households, the percentage of owner-occupied housing, and personal income per capita. The most significant of these is the percentage of female-headed households, which alone accounts for 25 percent of the variance. Of the remaining variables, two have signs opposite those expected, the percentage age 15 to 34 and the percentage living in poverty.

The addition of the capital punishment variables to the analysis of the full sample produces few changes (see table 6.2). The first three factors in both equations are the same, and the percentage of variance explained is identical. However, the number of inmates on death row enters as the fourth variable, and adds 2.9 percent to the level of statistical explanation. The remaining two variables in the equation also appeared in the first multiple regression, although their order has changed. Neither of them adds substantially to the predictive power of the model.

The significance of the capital punishment variable that enters the equation, however, is in its sign. The rate of violent crime is positively related to the number of inmates on death row. It certainly may be the case that the more violent areas produce more candidates for death row, but these data clearly do not support the position that placing people on death row or executing them is correlated with lower rates of violent crime.

The important tests for our purposes, however, are those that now include the capital punishment variables in the matched county pairs.

Table 6.1. Predictors of violent crime rate in 1,725 counties.

Variable	Beta	F	P	Mult. R^2	Inc. in R^2
%FEMHEAD	.436	267.892	.0001	.250	-----
%OWNHOME	-.285	79.214	.0001	.336	.086
PERCAPIN	.114	13.938	.0002	.364	.028
DENSITY	.062	7.697	.0056	.368	.004
%POVERTY	-.088	6.658	.0100	.370	.002
%15TO34	-.061	5.685	.0172	.372	.002

F-Ratio = 169.875, p = .0001

Table 6.2. Predictors of violent crime rate in 1,725 counties with capital punishment variables included.

Variable	Beta	F	P	Mult. R^2	Inc. in R^2
%FEMHEAD	.418	344.625	.0001	.250	-----
%OWNHOME	-.235	96.764	.0001	.336	.086
PERCAPIN	.069	5.3198	.0212	.364	.028
#DEATHROW	.194	102.716	.0001	.393	.029
%POVERTY	-.160	22.166	.0001	.400	.007
DENSITY	.090	17.985	.0001	.406	.006

F-Ratio = 195.56, p = .0001

To examine this, we have created independent or predictor variables that are computed as the *differences* between the matched counties on the variables used in the previous analyses, with the dependant variable computed as the difference in the county violent crime rates.

The t-test, commonly used to examine group differences, is inappropriate here because we are not concerned with the differences between the first counties as a group versus the second counties as a group. We are examining the effect that the difference between these variables in two specific counties has on determining the difference between those counties' violent crime levels. We are not concerned with comparing the means between two matched groups but are examining the differences between two counties on a case-by-case basis. Thus, the difference between the per capita income in Holmes County, Florida, compared to Geneva County, Alabama, is related directly to the difference between the violent crime rates in these same two counties.

These difference variables are employed as predictor variables in a regression, and the results appear in table 6.3. The most obvious finding for our research is that none of the capital punishment variables appear. In keeping with findings from other research, the difference in

Table 6.3. Socio-economic and capital punishment differences as predictors of differences in violent crime rates among 293 matched county pairs.

Variable	Beta	F	P	Mult. R^2	Inc. in R^2
Diff. DENSITY	.7613	501.05	.0001	.632	----
Diff. %FEMHEAD	.2354	33.00	.0001	.660	.028
Diff. INFTDEATH	-.1129	11.46	.0008	.675	.015
Diff. %POVERTY	-.1091	7.22	.0076	.683	.008

F Ratio = 155.360, p = .0001

population density between the two counties enters first (Decker and Kohfeld 1990; Kowalski and Duffield 1990), followed by the difference in the percentage of female headed households (see Sampson 1987), the difference in the infant death rate (see Loftin and Hill 1974), and the difference in the percentage below the poverty line (Bailey 1984a).

In order to examine the effect that the differences in the existence of capital punishment statutes, the number of people on death row, or the number of people executed since 1976 have on the difference in the violent crime rate in these matched counties, we forced the capital punishment variables into the equation first. Taken together, they produced an R^2 of .0176, in essence accounting for less than 2 percent of the variation. After these variables, the four factors reported above enter in the same order in roughly the same magnitude. Moreover, the relationship between the difference in the number of inmates on death row or the number executed and the difference in the violent crime rate in these matched pairs is again positive.

Conclusion and Discussion

There is, then, virtually no support here for a deterrence effect of capital punishment at the county level. Not the existence of a capital punishment statute at the state level, the presence of individuals on death row, nor the execution of individuals correlates with lower crime rates at the county level. Whatever the process for the deterrent effect of capital punishment is supposed to be—however the use of the death penalty at the state level is supposed to translate itself to individuals—it is not manifesting itself at the level of counties.

Indeed, what correlations do appear between capital punishment variables and violent crime are positive. As one increases, so does the other. Two arguments could account for our data. On the one hand, the data may support a just-deserts model. If there is more violent crime, there will be more people to sentence and execute, a logical or justified conclusion within that framework. On the other hand, a brutalization argument also fits the data. Two dimensions of this model could be relevant, both of which have also found empirical support in other research. It may be that frequent executions by the state create an atmosphere for the legitimation of violence, so that individuals come to decide for themselves that someone they personally define as a transgressor deserves to be killed (see Bowers 1988, 53). Another possibility is that increasing homicide rates may have the effect of fostering increased executions of offenders who are already waiting on death row (Bowers and Pierce 1980, 481–482). This research was designed to test the deterrence argument rather than evaluate brutalization effects or just-deserts, however, so while the data certainly fit a brutalization model better, we must be somewhat reserved in claims for support for that idea.

On the contrary, the deterrence model argues that the presence and enactment of capital punishment statutes will produce lowered levels of violent crime. Even if one suggests this will only occur over time, then the measure of the number of people executed by state since 1976 accounts for this difference. However, while our data provide some support for a brutalization or just-deserts argument, they clearly do not support deterrence as a function of capital punishment.

The positive correlation found also offers a strong challenge to a displacement argument. The contiguous counties we looked at offered excellent opportunities for displacement to occur; indeed, it is difficult to think of a more potentially ideal setting. The positive association between crime rates and the death penalty variables appears to dictate rejection of the idea that rational criminals move their activities from death penalty jurisdictions to non–death penalty jurisdictions when it is convenient to do so.

One of the more intriguing findings, albeit unrelated to the initial concerns of the study, is the predominance of the percentage of female headed households as a primary determinant of the level of violent crime at the county level, both in the general sample and in the smaller congruent-county sample. This is a finding that we can only suggest deserves further investigation, and we note that research by Sampson (1987), Messner and Sampson (1991), and Harries (1995) finds similar importance in the percentage of female households for certain types of crime, although LaFree, Drass, and O'Day (1992) find a negative effect from the same variable.

Taken together, our finding that sociodemographic factors are significant in predicting county-level rates of violent crime and the finding that the capital punishment variables are not significant again confirm the conclusion that structural factors and the cultural conditions that accompany them are far more important in determining the level of violent crime in a locality than are the actions of agencies of social control.

The decision of whether a model of justice based on a just-deserts philosophy is called for is a moral question and not one based upon data, since such a model does not rest on empirically testable beliefs that behaviors will change. Deterrence inherently rests on a belief that behavior will change and is, as a result, not supported. Whether a just-deserts model is justified by our findings may be a question for moral philosophy, theory, or politics. But our findings clearly offer no support for a deterrent effect of capital punishment.

7

The Life-Without-Parole Sanction

Probably the most commonly suggested alternative to the death penalty is the life-without-parole sentence, a topic first taken up in chapter 3 in the context of the emerging crisis in corrections that is arising out of the existence of large death row populations. Wright (1990, 1991) cited data suggesting that even in the more conservative states, a slight majority of the population might support restriction or abolition of capital punishment if a true life-without-parole sentence combined with a victim-restitution program were available. As table 7.1 shows, however, there is no clear relationship between the presence of a capital punishment provision in a state and a life-without-parole sentence. Twenty-six states had both (as of 1996), but 12 states with capital punishment had no life-without-parole option, and 8 states with life-without-parole sentences did not use the death penalty. That the geography of the sanction is to some extent nonrandom raises intriguing questions of cultural linkage that will be touched on later in the chapter.

Before the life-without-parole sentence is accepted as a viable alternative to capital punishment, it is important to examine three issues carefully.

First, what does the life-without-parole option really do, and how does it differ from a normal life sentence? *Second*, what is the impact of this alternative on the criminal justice system, and how substantial would this impact be if it were widely used as an alternative to capital punishment? *Third*, is this genuinely an alternative to a death sentence, or is it merely a harsher alternative to a normal life sentence?

We examine the first question by looking at what the life-without-parole sanction really is. The second question we approach by considering what the impact of the sentence would be on each agency of the criminal justice system. And the third question is considered by reviewing the geographic distribution of this sanction in combination with provisions for the death penalty.

Table 7.1. Life-without-parole (LWP) and capital punishment (CP) 1996, by states.

STATE	LWP	CP	STATE	LWP	CP
Alabama	Yes	Yes	Montana	Yes[2]	Yes
Alaska	No	No	Nebraska	Yes	Yes
Arizona	No	Yes	Nevada	Yes	Yes
Arkansas	Yes	Yes	New Hampshire	Yes	Yes
California	Yes	Yes	New Jersey	No	Yes
Colorado	No	Yes	New Mexico	No	Yes
Connecticut	Yes	Yes	New York	No	Yes
Delaware	Yes	Yes	N. Carolina	No	Yes
Florida	Yes	Yes	North Dakota	No	No
Georgia	Yes	Yes	Ohio	No	Yes
Hawaii	Yes	No	Oklahoma	Yes	Yes
Idaho	Yes[1]	Yes	Oregon	Yes	Yes
Illinois	Yes	Yes	Pennsylvania	Yes[1]	Yes
Indiana	No	Yes	Rhode Island	Yes	No
Iowa	Yes	No	S. Carolina	Yes[3]	Yes
Kansas	No	Yes	South Dakota	Yes[1]	Yes
Kentucky	No	Yes	Tennessee	No	Yes
Louisiana	Yes	Yes	Texas	No	Yes
Maine	Yes	No	Utah	Yes	Yes
Maryland	Yes	Yes	Vermont	Yes	No
Massachusetts	Yes	No	Virginia	Yes[1]	Yes
Michigan	Yes[1]	No	Washington	Yes	Yes
Minnesota	No	No	West Virginia	Yes	No
Mississippi	Yes	Yes	Wisconsin	No	No
Missouri	Yes	Yes	Wyoming	Yes[1]	Yes

[1] Contained in parole sections.
[2] May be applied to any sentence over one year.
[3] Applies only on a commuted death sentence (see Wright 1990, 546).

The Life-Without-Parole Sanction: What Is It?

Fundamentally, a life sentence is an attempt on the part of the members of a society to banish from their community one of their number for the remainder of his or her natural life. In this century that sentence has characteristically been applied only to the most recalcitrant or dangerous criminals. However, evidence suggests increasing public frustration that follows from the awareness that a life sentence may not, in fact, remove an offender from society for life (U.S. Department of Justice 1985b). Although the public perception of this as leniency may be, as Doleschal (1979) notes, "the triumph of folklore over fact," the polls show a steady increase in the percentage of the American population that feels that the courts do not deal harshly enough with criminals (U.S. Department of Justice 1986; see also Glick and Pruet 1985, 319–324 for a review of the literature on public opinion regarding judicial leniency). Life-without-parole sentences appear to be attempts to change that perception. Yet these statutes are not all that the public or practitioners in the field assume them to be. They may not, in fact, guarantee life without any possibility of release.

In the vast majority of the states with life-without-parole statutes, the sanction is applied for a single crime, most commonly first-degree murder, rather than for any pattern of criminal behavior. Since the majority of these statutes apply to first-degree murder, they have been referred to as capital offender statutes and are relevant to the question of the use of capital punishment. A second form of life-without-parole statute focuses on habitual offenders. In these cases the offender need not be a particularly violent or dangerous criminal, but he or she must have a record of repeated criminal offenses indicating an unwillingness to conform to the criminal law. The central feature of these laws is the enhancement of the sanction for the current offense. These statutes are designed to deal with the problem of the habitual or career criminal and as such are not directly relevant to life-without-parole as it relates to the issue of capital punishment.

Capital-Offender Life-Without-Parole Statutes

With minor variations in each state, these statutes are similar in their construction. In six states the specific provision for life without parole is contained in those sections of the criminal code dealing with the duties and responsibilities of the parole board or parole commission. Characteristically, the statute notes that the parole agency has normal parole powers except in certain cases and then specifies those cases. Pennsylvania's legislation is characteristic of this approach, and notes simply that the parole board "is hereby authorized to release on parole any convict . . . except convicts condemned to death or serving life imprisonment" (Pa. Stat. Ann. §331.221, Purdon, 1964). This approach to restricting parole in life sentences tends to be rather broad, constraining the board's authority in any case where the sentence is life imprisonment.

More commonly, life-without-parole is a sanction for specified forms of first-degree murder. The penalty may be an alternative to capital punishment or to a normal life sentence, depending upon the aggravating and mitigating circumstances of the offense and offender. The general features of the provision can be seen in Nevada's statute:

> Every person convicted of murder of the first degree shall be punished: (a) By death, only if one or more aggravating circumstances are found and any mitigating circumstance or circumstances which are found do not outweigh the aggravating circumstance or circumstances. (b) Otherwise, by imprisonment in the state prison for life with or without possibility of parole. If the penalty is fixed at life imprisonment with possibility of parole, eligibility for parole begins when a minimum of 10 years has been served. (Nev. Rev. Stat. § 220.030, 1983)

The states vary on the issues of aggravating or mitigating circumstances, in ways that often reflect the presence or absence of the death penalty in that state. In states without capital punishment, the sanction is automatic if an offender is found guilty of first-degree murder, of specific forms of murder, or of murder occurring under specific circumstances, depending upon the particular state code. Only lesser degrees of homicide, or, as in West Virginia, the specific recommendation for mercy by the jury, can allow for parole. In states with capital punishment, life-without-parole may either be an alternative to be considered by the court after weighing the circumstances of the case or may be an automatic sentence if the death penalty is not given. Wright (1990) presents a full description of the various legal forms the relationship can take among capital punishment, the life-without-parole sanction, and the traditional life sentence.

In only one state, Montana, does the sanction appear to be so broad as to apply to a full variety of people and crimes. There, the sanction is among the additional restrictions on sentences that may be considered "necessary to obtain the objectives of rehabilitation and the protection of society" (Mont. Code Ann. § 46-18-202, 1985). Montana's provision serves as a clear statement of the primary purpose of any life-without-release sanction, and the following section of that statute is quoted in full for that reason.

The Life-Without-Parole Sanction

> Whenever the district court imposes a sentence of imprisonment in the state prison for a term exceeding one year, the court may also impose the restriction that the defendant be ineligible for parole and participation in the supervised release program while serving his term. If such a restriction is to be imposed, the court shall state the reasons for it in writing. If the court finds that the restriction is necessary for the protection of society, it shall impose the restriction as part of the sentence and the judgement shall contain a statement of the reasons for the restriction. (Mont. Code Ann. § 46-18-202, 1985)

While the capital offender statutes clearly reflect a just-deserts model and a punitive stance, deterrence also appears to be a major emphasis in these life-without-parole sentences. Although the probability of continued criminal behavior may be low among murderers in general compared to other criminal offenders, the offenders targeted by these statutes are not "ordinary" murderers. Almost all capital offender statutes note that the particular act involved must have been particularly heinous, cruel, or otherwise out of the ordinary. In these cases, the nature of the act is such that the community does not wish to take any risk, however slight, that such a crime might be repeated by the offender.

At present no empirical studies have examined the factors leading to the passage of capital offender statutes. However, in interviews with representatives of the state's attorney's or attorney general's offices from states with capital offender statutes, those who discussed the evolution and passage of these laws commonly perceived that they were legislated quickly and often rather abruptly, characteristically in response to a particular murder or other heinous criminal act, and commonly through the action of a particular person or small group of people. These people were in some cases relatives of the victim of the murder.

The degree to which such moral entrepreneurs are necessary for the passage of these kinds of laws is an interesting empirical question touched upon in Stewart and Lieberman's (1982) review of the life-without-parole sentence. The public seems to be increasingly aware that a life sentence does not mean that the offender will be incarcerated for life, and it is likely that this public understanding is a necessary prior condition for passage of a capital offender life-without-parole statute. A specific murder that leaves a politically astute or fully committed relative of the victim as the moral entrepreneur serves as the precipitating event to the passage of such a bill. Given that, these statutes may become even more common as acts of violence continue to occur and as long as the just-deserts model remains in favor.

The Life-Without-Parole Sentence and the Reality of Commutation

Life-without-parole statutes are characteristically written to eliminate the possibility of release through the more common channels of parole or expiration of sentence (possible in some cases due to provision for "good time" consideration). In some instances, even the possibility of work-release or educational furlough is excluded. Only one state, however, seems to recognize the full range of possibilities for release and addresses that range in some detail. The Washington state statute is unusually specific in its provisions.

> A person sentenced to life imprisonment under this section shall not have that sentence suspended, deferred, or commuted by any judicial officer and the board of prison terms and paroles or its successor may not parole such prisoner nor reduce the period of confinement in any manner whatsoever including but not limited to any sort of good-time calculation. The department of social and health services or its successor or any executive official may not permit such prisoner to participate in any sort of release or furlough program. (Wash. Rev. Code Ann. §10.95.030, 1986)

Legislatures appear to be differentially aware of the varieties of alternative forms of release or are differentially willing to consider this question. The issue of executive commutation, in particular, is seldom directly addressed. Yet from her study of commutation practices, Martin has concluded:

> As states return to determinate sentencing structures, the importance of executive clemency is likely to increase, as it again provides a mechanism for dealing with problems of prison crowding, inflexible and disparate sentences, and management of growing numbers of prisoners with life and long-term sentences. (Martin 1983, 594)

Forty-eight states have granted variations of some form of commutation powers to the executive. To fully guarantee by legislative action that an offender would have no opportunity for release under any circumstances would challenge the constitutional powers of clemency lodged with the executive by these states. However, Martin noted that changes over the past two decades have restrained the free employment of commutations by governors. In addition to increased emphasis on public notification of clemency applications and a decentralization of clemency authority, three trends are apparent.

> First, use of commutation to reduce prison populations . . . second, development of . . . standards to guide application and decision making . . . and

third, a reduction in the proportion and/or number of regular applications that result in commutations where a "tough on crime" policy generally prevails in a state. (Martin 1983, 608)

This capacity of the executive to pardon may be the last resort to avoid two unpleasant realities that occur in life-without-parole cases. First, the individuals sentenced will eventually grow old. Commutation provides a mechanism for release of the old, infirm, and no longer dangerous offender. Second, commutation serves as an essential tool in dealing with the universal plague of overcrowding (see Martin 1983, 604–606). The existence of a safety valve via commutation, cumbersome and politically sensitive as it may be, is not something a state's executive will willingly dispense with (Martin 1983, 610).

As a result, commutation will probably continue to be an available avenue for release, even for those individuals with life-without-parole sentences, and it is unlikely that this possibility will be removed by legislative action. As long as the life-without-parole sanction is applied to relatively small numbers of people and their sentences are commuted quietly after 20 or more years, it is probable that there will be no great public outcry against this method of release.

The Impact of the Life-Without-Parole Sentence on the Criminal Justice System

The life-without-parole sanction has a major impact on corrections and prosecution within the criminal justice system. Certainly, the provision provides judges with another alternative for consideration in sentencing, but the sanction does not affect the structure of the judiciary nor change the way in which the judiciary operates. Much the same is true for the police. While police departments may choose to enhance their efforts in these cases and may establish special career criminal units or teams to work with prosecutors, the existence of the life-without-parole statute will not inevitably affect police operations. (See National Institute of Justice 1986 for a discussion of police responses to career criminal provisions.)

The ability to decide within an agency how much of an impact the presence of a life-without-parole provision will have for that agency is a luxury less available for prosecutors than for police and is largely out of the hands of corrections agencies. This sentencing alternative simply adds one more variable to the considerations undertaken by the judge or jury. As such, it changes the negotiations that the prosecution can carry on with defendant and judge and also changes the dynamics of prosecution and defense in the courtroom drama played out for the judge and jury.

The presence of a life-without-parole statute will inevitably cause such changes. Indeed, the defense will guarantee that they will happen in capital cases. However, prosecutors will still have the option to react to this as they choose. In other words, changes in prosecution where life-without-parole statutes already exist or are passed in the future will depend in large part on the professional and prosecutorial skills of the attorneys involved (Foley and Powell 1982).

For attorneys, these changes will be most apparent in states with both the death penalty and a life-without-parole option. A recommendation of life-without-parole by a jury, or such a decision by the judge, will avoid condemning another human being to death. If such a decision appears to be the best that a defense attorney can hope for, then all of her or his skills will be focused on that outcome. The research on this discretion in capital cases seems to indicate that the ability to purchase the skills or additional time available from a private attorney may introduce an unanticipated bias into judgments in cases in states with both the death penalty and life-without-parole (Foley and Powell 1982). In those cases where the prosecutor feels the death penalty is appropriate, she or he will have to deal with the possibility that the judge or jury can compromise to life-without-parole if such a sanction is available.

But it is undoubtedly on the correctional system that the life-without-parole sanction will have the greatest impact. Its increased use either as an alternative to capital punishment or as a more stringent form of a life sentence will obviously increase the number of inmates with this sentence in the correctional system. The growth in numbers of such prisoners will have both short-term and long-term consequences. In the immediate future, the security problems of institutions charged with their control is a significant question for corrections (see Cheatwood 1985, 470–477). In the long run, the major effect of an increased use of this sentence will be in the changing nature of the inmate population balance, specifically the growth of a large segment of the inmate population that is significantly older than the prison population in general.

Geometric Growth of the Prison Population

Underlying both the short-term and long-term problems is the geometric growth of this group within the inmate population. The percentage of life-without-release prisoners as a percentage of the total inmate population will continue to increase, even if the percentage of commitments they represent remains constant.

This is fairly simple to demonstrate. Based on data from the U.S. Department of Justice, 23.5 percent of all inmates sentenced to life will be released within 3 years, 44.3 percent will be released within 5 years,

58.8 percent within 7 years, and 77.0 percent within 10 years of their commitment (U.S. Department of Justice 1985a). Yet those with life-without-parole sentences remain, and their proportions of all inmates slowly increase, even if the proportion of those convicted who *receive* that sentence remains constant.

For *each 1 percent* of the committed population that has a life-without-parole sentence, the actual percentage of the correctional population at the end of three years with such a sentence will be 1.25 percent. At the end of 5 years this will have grown to 1.4 percent, and after 10 years this 1 percent rate of increase will account for 1.8 percent of the prison population. The problem will get progressively worse as time passes. If half of the normal "lifers" are released between 3 and 5 years and over two-thirds are out by 10 years after sentence, an increasing proportion of the "lifers" remaining in the institution will be life-without-parole inmates. After 40 years, as these inmates near and exceed age 65, each 1 percent originally sentenced to a life-without-parole term will have come to represent approximately 5.8 percent of the life sentence population in prison.

Security Issues

There is, of course, the danger that the widespread use of the life-without-parole sentence may initially create what Stewart and Lieberman (1982) call a "new breed of superinmates, prone to violence and uncontrollable." Certainly, since its inception, the idea of parole has been a mainstay of institutional control, and removal of the control that the promise of early release affords an institution may leave nothing to use as a sanction for dangerous or disruptive behaviors.

But some officials with experience in dealing with such inmates do not feel that they pose a qualitatively different security threat. While the life-without-parole inmate certainly has less chance for normal release than others, these officials argue that maximum-security procedures are already designed to hold and control dangerous inmates. Jerry Springborn, clinical services supervisor at the Stateville, Illinois, penitentiary noted, "such usual prison disciplinary tools as loss of privilege and isolation are useful in controlling all types of inmates," and he observed no significant differences in the more than 15 life-without-parole inmates at Stateville (quoted in Stewart and Lieberman 1982, 16–17). Robert Dickover in California made the same observation and doubted "that they pose anymore of a problem than others committed with a likelihood for parole."[1]

However, this perspective is not universally shared. Dean Leach, executive assistant to the warden of the Marion Federal Penitentiary, noted that these offenders require individual cells, segregated recreation areas, and larger staff: "You can't just mingle these people in the population without problems."[2] This dilemma affects daily operations ranging from living and working assignments to simple inmate movement, and unquestionably makes prison operation more problematic. But the comments of Ed Carnes, Alabama assistant attorney general, are thoughtful and to the point in this regard: "It's a choice between them committing offenses on the street or giving prison officials a hard time. We're more concerned with how they behave out on the street" (quoted in Stewart and Lieberman 1982, 16).

If these individuals are as likely to maintain a career of violence on the streets as they are in the correctional institution, penal institutions are unquestionably better suited to control and protect themselves against such people.

As these laws are being passed now, the image of the offender against whom they are directed is a young, vicious, and dangerous predator whom society cannot allow in its midst. Security must work with that image in mind. But the long-term problem for corrections is with the growth and graying of this population. In the future we must begin to work with the image of burned-out, sick old men. That will be the reality of life-without-parole within a few decades.

The Increasing Elderly Inmate Population

The impact of an increasingly elderly segment of the inmate population will force qualitative changes, not merely simple quantitative increases, in certain services or facilities. A well-staffed infirmary or hospital in a prison of 500 to 1,000 inmates may be able to accommodate 5 or so elderly inmates without major changes in staffing or facilities. However, as the number of elderly inmates increases, more demands appear that cannot be met with a mere increase in standard staff and facilities. Strains will be placed on the health care facilities, the physical plant, the staff, and on the general social and psychological state of the inmates and the staff working in these settings. Someone in correctional departments with large populations has to begin to think in terms of maximum-security convalescent homes.

Some quick observations on the research in this area indicate the extent of the problem. Morton and Anderson (1983) pointed out that around 75 percent of all older people have some form of chronic health disorder, and Wilson and Vito (1986) found that the elderly population in the prison that they examined had a greater percentage of individuals with serious health problems (20.3 percent) than did the general inmate population (3.2 percent). McCarthy's (1983) study of 248 elderly offenders in the Florida correctional system found that 15.3 percent had been ill at least 22 days in the prior month, and 10.5 percent of the total were confined to bed.

Even if we assume that the health of older inmates is, ironically, better than that of their free counterparts (see Reed and Glasmer 1979), these figures still indicate that 25 percent of the elderly inmates need almost constant medical attention. Studies of the elderly inmate population in Maryland by Chaiklin and Fultz (1985) found that the common ailments of old age plagued the inmates and that fully 95 percent of the population required medication.

If the chronically ill older inmate/patient is kept at the institution, the potential stress on limited bed space and on budget is substantial. In one study, only six older inmates (aged 68 or older) were kept at the Maryland Penitentiary, for example, yet two of these six had to be permanently housed in the hospital. Those two used 15 percent of all available space in the hospital (Chaiklin and Fultz 1985). The aging process proceeds inexorably for everyone, including inmates. Since the chances of developing debilitating illnesses increase dramatically with age, if only two more of their cohort become bedridden, 30 percent of all hospital space in that penitentiary would be occupied by chronically ill elderly inmates.

The conclusion of those who have examined the problem is that the needs of the elderly are at least as great, if not greater, than the needs of the general inmate population. Yet Chaiklin and Fultz offered the pessimistic conclusion that we are ill-prepared to deal with the older offender. "The literature on the aged offender," they wrote, "does not develop a comprehensive picture of who they are as individuals, what their needs are, and how they could be helped while in prison" (1985, 26).

Is Life-Without-Parole an Alternative to Life or to Death?

Out of these rather pessimistic views of the future of life-without-parole, is there any solace in discovering whether the sanction is at least a more humane option to capital punishment or whether it is rather a more severe form of a life sentence?

Non-Random Geography and the Issue of Cultural Linkage

If life-without-parole is seen as a less severe alternative to capital punishment, then we would expect to see this alternative more available in those areas of the country that have been less enthusiastic in their past application of the death penalty. This would imply that we would expect to see more states with capital punishment *and* with life-without-parole in the Northeast and the Midwest. On the other hand, if life-without-parole is seen as a more stringent form of life, to be used in concert with the death penalty, we would expect to find more states with both provisions in the traditionally harsher South and West.

The geography of the relationship illustrates and clarifies associations between capital punishment and life-without-parole, and addresses the assumptions posed above (figure 7.1). The map displays the relationships between the death penalty and life-without-parole statutes by state. Clearly, the South and far West dominate among those states having both penalties. This certainly suggests that the life-without-parole sanction is being employed as a harsher form of life rather than as a less harsh alternative to death. There are some outliers. Texas, North Carolina, and Tennessee are all southern states with capital punishment but without life-without-parole

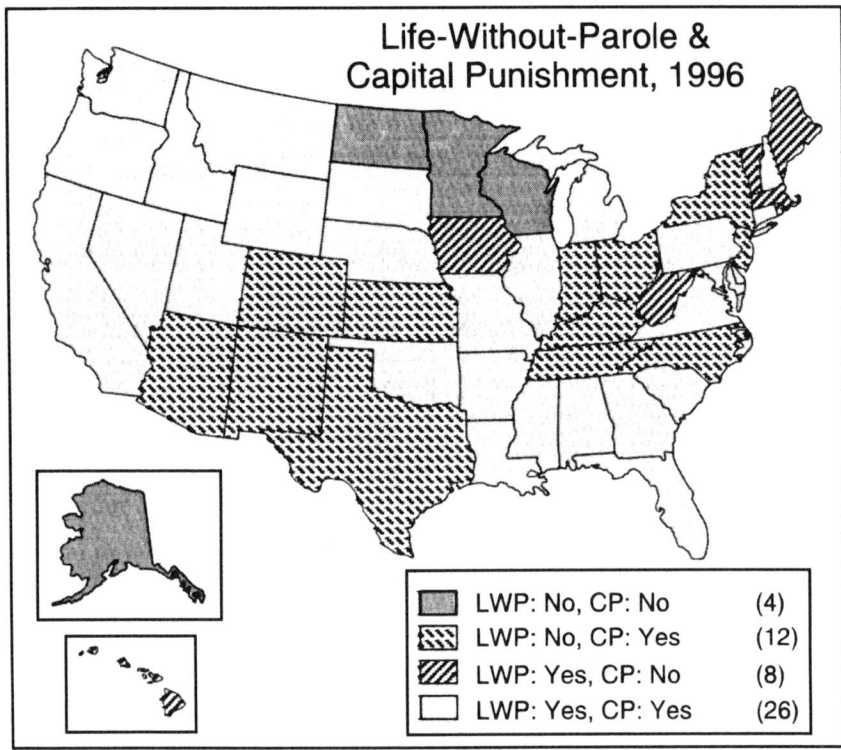

Figure 7.1. Life-without-parole and capital punishment, 1996, by states. *Souce*: authors.

statutes, and Pennsylvania, Connecticut, and New Hampshire are northeastern states that have both sanctions. Yet overall, the pattern remains that of the southern and western states having both forms of penalties, and the northeastern and midwestern states having life-without-parole without capital punishment, or neither provision, in their laws.

In short, *the geographic distribution of the life-without-parole laws in combination with death penalty laws certainly supports the contention that life-without-parole is more of an alternative to a normal life sentence than an alternative to the death penalty.* Significantly, the geography also brings into question the genuineness of the "good-will" implied in surveys suggesting that state electorates would support the revision or abolition of capital punishment if life-without-parole were an alternative.

Life-Without-Parole: What We Need to Know

We need to have some idea of the origin of the life-without-parole laws and the real impact that the increased use of this sanction may have if we are to have any hope of avoiding some of its potential major problems. *First*, study of the formulation and passage of these laws could provide us with increased understanding of the social and political processes by which statutes in such emotionally charged areas are enacted. To understand the process by which these laws are passed, we will have to turn to case studies of states that have recently passed capital offender life-without-parole statutes. These statutes appear to be the products of single, landmark violent crimes. As such, they may serve as benchmark case studies of the role of the media, of the moral entrepreneur, and of small but committed groups on the legislative process as it relates to emotionally charged issues.

Second, we should continue our examination of the impact of life-without-parole laws on prosecutorial offices and the procedures by which these offices attempt to carry out the mandate of the law. In those states with capital punishment, we need to consider what the effect of a life-without-parole sentence may be on the possibility of securing death sentences. We do not know which of the systems established among the various prosecutorial units and the various states is most effective. Yet if state legislatures pass such laws and expect them to be enforced, these questions must be addressed.

Third, we must examine the administrative and managerial problems that the increase in a life-without-parole population creates for corrections systems. We must continue to monitor the monetary cost of an increasing segment of older inmates and the medical and support needs of this segment of the prison population. (See Sigler and Culliver 1988 for such an initial attempt.) It is of central importance to determine at what point the existing system will become inadequate and what sort of facility will be necessary to accommodate these offenders. The research and policy-related conclusions by Wilson and Vito (1986, 19–27) constitute a case study of the potential of this approach.

Fourth, we should address the basic question of how much more violent or troublesome, if they are at all, a life-without-parole population will be if the option becomes a serious alternative to capital punishment.

It may be that life-without-parole is simply another fad in criminal justice, another attempt by a public frustrated with crime to do something about the problem. It may be that the sentence and the inmates with the sentence will simply be integrated into the ongoing process, with the various actors in the system accommodating themselves to the change and its impact. It is almost certainly the case that in trying to solve a very genuine social problem, we will create a new set of problems in a classic replay of unintended consequences.

Legal Cases and State Codes Cited

California v. Ramos, 103 S.Ct. 3446 (1983).
Montana. 1985. Montana Code Annotated, § 46-18-202.
Nevada. 1983. Nevada Revised Statutes, § 220.030 (1983).
Pennsylvania. 1964. Purdon's Pennsylvania Statutes Annotated, § 331.21.
Solem v. Helm, 103 S.Ct. 3001 (1983).
Washington. 1986 supp. Revised Code of Washington Annotated, § 10.95.030.

Notes

1. Quotes from Robert Dickover, research program specialist for the California Department of Corrections, are taken from a telephone interview, February 1984.

2. Quotes from Dean Leach are taken from a telephone interview in March 1984.

8

Epilogue

Business As Usual?

As a fundamentally violent culture with persistently high rates of violent crime throughout its history, the United States is set apart from other developed countries. As a result, it would seem to be positioned to continue to use capital punishment in the foreseeable future in response to public demands to provide punishment commensurate with that high level of lethal violence. As noted in chapter 1, whether the rate of executions will increase to the levels of the peak era is debatable. While the public tends to approve the concept of execution, and politicians are under considerable pressure to increase the rate of capital punishment, there is also an undercurrent of realization to the effect that it is essentially impossible to administer capital punishment fairly, and, efforts at "reform" notwithstanding, considerable evidence continues to point to levels of execution of African-Americans at excessive rates, even taking into account their overrepresentation in the offender pool (Margolick 1991; Raspberry 1994).

Scope for Further Research

Given the prominence of capital punishment on the public policy agenda in the United States, and the lack of definitive answers to several questions, considerable scope remains for further geographic research. For example, intrastate geography of capital punishment, conducted at the county level, could demonstrate more clearly than hitherto how variations in prosecutorial discretion and such factors as the election of judges, jury sentencing, the characteristics of the public defender system, the prevalence of plea bargaining, and the dynamics of victim-offender relationships (including their racial composition) affect outcomes in capital cases.[1]

Such relationships were vividly illustrated by a conflict in New York City that pitted Governor George E. Pataki, a Republican who had campaigned on the promise to restore the death penalty in New York, against Bronx District Attorney Robert T. Johnson. Pataki removed Johnson as the prosecutor of a paroled convict accused of killing a police officer in a shootout on Grand Concourse, the main street of the Bronx. Pataki was convinced that Johnson would not seek the death penalty, about which he had expressed moral and ethical objections. (Johnson was influenced in part by having been successful in a murder prosecution in which the person convicted was later found to be innocent.) An interesting twist was that the defendant might have been presented with grounds for appeal based on the governor's coercion of the system (Goshko 1996).

Changes Working Through the System

As the twentieth century draws to its conclusion, some of the geographically specific changes in capital punishment procedures that have moved more or less sluggishly through state legislatures over the last decade are beginning to have their effects. In September 1995, the *Washington Post* reported that Virginia had scheduled nine executions in the last three months of the year, "an unprecedented schedule even for a state that uses its death chamber more than most, and a reflection of a national movement toward swifter executions" (Baker 1995). Like other aspects of capital punishment, the move to hasten executions is much further along in some states than others, reinforcing the concept of a distinct geography of capital punishment and raising the specter not only of a substantially increased number of executions, but also of an increasing number of executions of innocent persons.

While the simple arithmetic of the numbers on death row, in combination with the political climate, makes it difficult to see anything other than escalating levels of capital punishment in the foreseeable future, another ominous but less conspicuous factor is that death penalty resource centers are shutting down owing to budget cuts, and it has been these resource centers that have provided lawyers to assist death row residents who are typically without the wherewithal to retain an attorney who might have capital case experience.

Public Defender Decline

In Florida, for example, free legal counsel is given death-sentenced prisoners only through the first appeal at the state level (Von Drehle 1995c, 138). The *Washington Post* noted that two states, Mississippi and Alabama, paid lawyers only $1,000 to deal with the entire trial and appeal process. Given that a typical fee rate for lawyers is $150–200 per hour, this would translate into less than seven hours of "real" legal services and would be hopelessly inadequate as a proper defense, in view of the need for a legal team to spend literally thousands of hours in such cases. "Worse yet," noted the *Post*, "a recent study found cases in which a defense attorney had failed to read the state's death penalty statute or dozed through parts of a capital murder trial. In a case in Alabama, an attorney had shown up for trial so drunk that he was jailed for contempt" (Torry 1996).

In view of the fact that nearly half of the cases reviewed in federal courts lead to the overturning of death sentences or convictions (Torry 1996), the prospective elimination or drastic reduction in legal services would seem likely to lead not only to more executions more quickly, but also to a much higher rate of error. Just the task of getting lawyers to represent death row prisoners is getting out of hand, now that national death row population is over 3,000. In Florida alone, Von Drehle likened the task of engaging lawyers for the condemned to "bailing out the *Titanic* with a teaspoon" and noted that Florida actually had already had to confront, in 1985, the question of whether the state would execute an unrepresented prisoner (Von Drehle 1996c, 138, 277).

Will the Floodgates Open?

It is against this backdrop of the—as yet not entirely realized—threat of the "opening of the floodgates" that we write this epilogue. For proponents of the death penalty, this is a grand prospect, for opponents, a ghastly one. As we have already pointed out, the issue is ultimately a moral one, analogous, perhaps, to the abortion issue, with hard battle lines and few minds changed over time. In chapters 3 and 7 we attempted to sketch some of the possible scenarios as death row (and life-without-parole) populations increase and executions become more frequent—perhaps so frequent that a backlash against capital punishment will develop. For the moment, at least, it seems that revenge is increasing in importance as a socially acceptable justification for capital punishment; seven states now allow victims' families as witnesses to executions. In Huntsville, Texas, Linda Kelley reported that the experience of seeing Leo Jenkins, who had shot her two children in a pawnshop robbery in Houston, die by lethal injection, was "immensely satisfying" (Pressley 1996). If deterrence goes away as an "official" justification for capital punishment, vengeance may come to the fore as the principal policy rationale, one that has evidently been rejected in most of the rest of the developed world. As Cohen (1996) asked, "Should the state be in the revenge business?"

Another dimension of the renaissance of capital punishment now under way is the untested possibility that very large numbers of executions—several hundred in a given year—*may* have a deterrent effect. Ironically, however, executions on such a scale would use up the available death row populations quite rapidly, thus soon *eliminating* the possible deterrent.

Persistence of Geographic Variation

While no one can predict the outcome with any certainty, we can be sure that *geographic* variations in the treatment of those who kill, or who are accused of killing, will persist. Laws will continue to vary; some states will have capital statutes, some will not. The specifics of state laws will differ at least with respect to the details of aggravating and mitigating circumstances and with regard to the basic qualification for capital consideration—double homicide, for example. The existing structure of state-determined laws ensures that similar people committing similar crimes will be treated differently, a situation that reaches a critical pitch when the difference is a matter of life and death, as it often is (figure 1.1).

Perfect geographic equality is, of course, unattainable, and many would no doubt argue that it is also undesirable. (How can local and regional cultural preferences be expressed, if that is the democratically arrived at desire of the citizens, if laws do not vary?) Even in countries with central, nonfederal systems of government, there is place-to-place variation in the treatment of lawbreakers and alleged lawbreakers. The crucial question, perhaps, is: What level of variation is acceptable before the principle of equal protection under the law is so grossly breached that the law itself becomes a source of ridicule and the system runs the risk of collapsing under the weight of its own injustice?

Moral Authority

As we noted at the outset, the United States will be pedaling uphill in terms of opinion in the developed world if the much-anticipated opening of the floodgates of execution does indeed happen. It is likely that the court of world opinion will increasingly liken the United States to China, Iran, and Nigeria, and the phrase "violation of human rights," generally used as a diplomatic weapon directed against repressive Third World regimes, will be turned against the United States, undermining what might be loosely termed its "moral authority." This risk

Epilogue

should be weighed against the satisfaction that death penalty proponents will derive from wholesale executions, and the corresponding rewards that may accrue to politicians who are in positions allowing them to take credit for employing what some regard as the ultimate deterrent.

Notes

1. For further discussion of these factors in a geographic context, see Harries and Brunn 1978.

Appendix I

Changes in the Espy File Between 1986 and 1995

Note: That a map shows increase means only that the *confirmations* in the Espy File increased between 1986 and 1995, not necessarily that executions actually occurred in those states in that time period (e.g., Wisconsin).

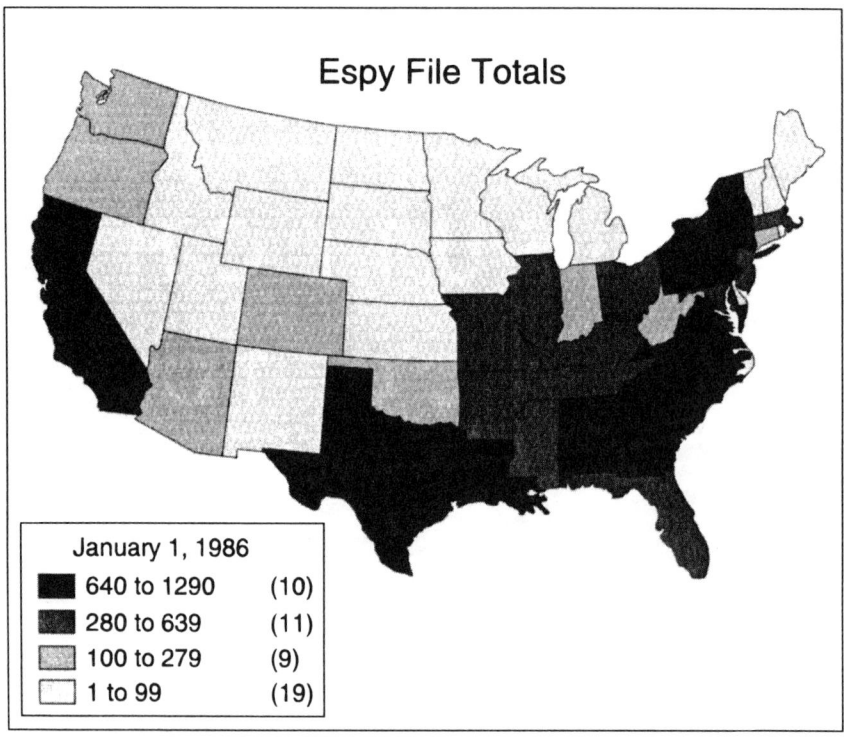

Figure A1. Espy File totals, 1 January, 1986, by states.

Changes in the Espy File Between 1986 and 1995

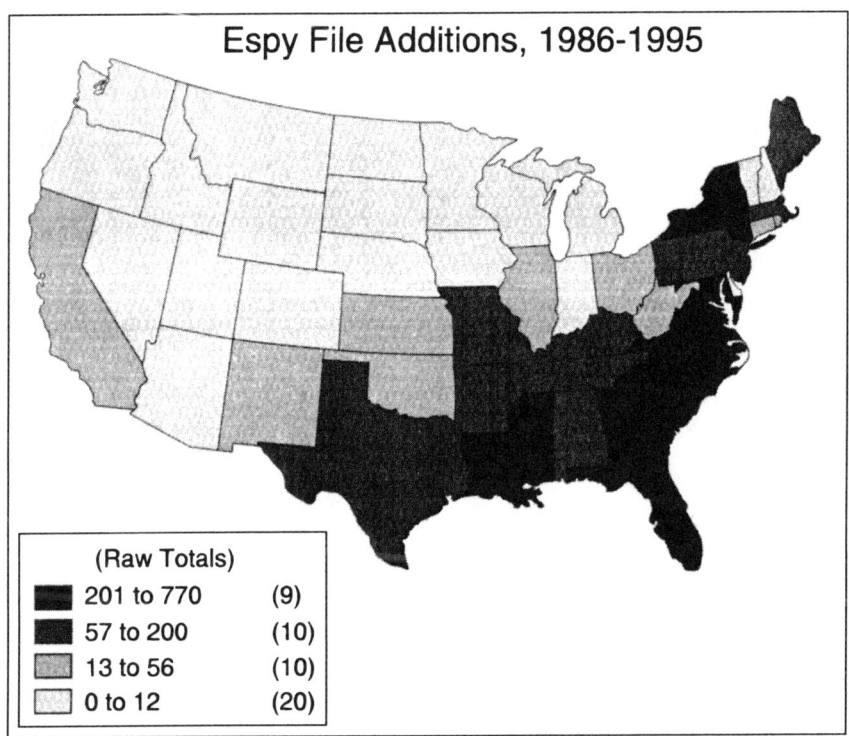

Figure A2. Espy File additions, 1986–1995. Raw totals, by states.

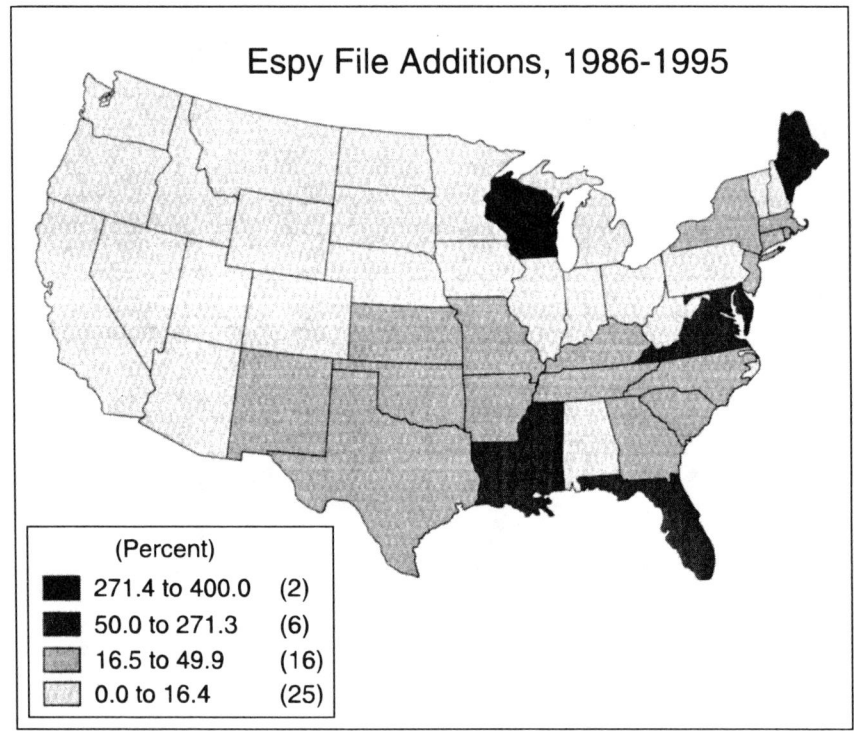

Figure A3. Espy File additions, 1986–1995, as percentage of pre-1986 totals, by states.

Appendix II

States and Their Methods of Execution

See figure 2.8 for a mapped version of these data.
These 38 states allow executions by the following means:

Alabama:	Electrocution
Arizona:	Gas chamber, lethal injection
Arkansas:	Electrocution, lethal injection
California:	Gas chamber, lethal injection
Colorado:	Lethal injection
Delaware:	Lethal injection
Florida:	Electrocution
Georgia:	Electrocution
Idaho:	Firing squad, lethal injection
Illinois:	Lethal injection
Indiana:	Electrocution
Kansas:	Lethal injection
Kentucky:	Electrocution
Louisiana:	Lethal injection
Maryland:	Gas chamber
Mississippi:	Gas chamber, lethal injection
Missouri:	Lethal injection

Montana:	Hanging, lethal injection
Nebraska:	Electrocution
Nevada:	Lethal injection
New Hampshire:	Lethal injection
New Jersey:	Lethal injection
New Mexico:	Lethal injection
New York:	Lethal injection
North Carolina:	Gas chamber, lethal injection
Ohio:	Electrocution, lethal injection
Oklahoma:	Lethal injection
Oregon:	Lethal injection
Pennsylvania:	Lethal injection
Rhode Island:	Electrocution
South Carolina:	Electrocution
South Dakota:	Lethal injection
Tennessee:	Electrocution
Texas:	Lethal injection
Utah:	Firing squad, lethal injection
Virginia:	Electrocution, lethal injection
Washington:	Hanging, lethal injection
Wyoming:	Lethal injection

These methods of execution are used in the following states:

Electrocution: Alabama, Arkansas, Florida, Georgia, Indiana, Kentucky, Nebraska, Ohio, Rhode Island, South Carolina, Tennessee, Virginia
Firing Squad: Idaho, Utah
Gas Chamber: Arizona, California, Maryland, Mississippi, North Carolina
Hanging: Montana, Washington
Lethal Injection: Arizona, Arkansas, California, Colorado, Delaware, Idaho, Illinois, Kansas, Louisiana, Mississippi, Missouri,

Montana, Nevada, New Hampshire, New Jersey, New Mexico, North Carolina, Ohio, Oklahoma, Oregon, Pennsylvania, South Dakota, Texas, Utah, Virginia, Washington, Wyoming

These 12 states (plus Washington, D.C.) have no death penalty:

Alaska
Washington, D.C.
Hawaii
Iowa
Maine
Massachusetts
Michigan
Minnesota
North Dakota
Rhode Island
Vermont
West Virginia
Wisconsin

Source: Death Penalty Information Center, 9 January, 1996.

Appendix III

Technical Notes

Overview

The analysis on which this book is based employed a combination of newly generated and archived data sets. For the most part, either SAS[1] (Statistical Analysis System) or SPSS[2] (Statistical Package for the Social Sciences) were used to generate the various statistics or summaries presented or to pre-process data for later introduction into desktop mapping. The package used for mapping was MapInfo.[3] Most charts and diagrams were also done in MapInfo. A few were prepared in Microsoft Excel. The determinant was simply that the program that happened to be at hand was the most likely to be used, given that charting software has tended to converge, and most programs now have similar capabilities.

Much of what has been done here could be replicated or extended through the use of the same data, much of which is available through the Inter-university Consortium for Political and Social Research[4] (ICPSR), to which most research universities belong. Such analysis could form the basis of exercises in courses in several social science disciplines. Co-author Keith Harries has employed this approach in a senior-level course in social geography in which students did background reading in order to gain theoretical insights, developed a problem (hypothesis), and then used archived data in conjunction with SAS, proprietary digital base maps (states, counties, or city streets), and desktop mapping software in order to "spatially enable" the data, that is, make it mappable and amenable to specifically *spatial* analysis. This process permits the creation of geographic visualizations (maps), some of which employed a geographic information systems (GIS) approach involving the layering of data in order to reveal spatial relationships. Spatial enabling also permits such manipulations as the counting of events ("objects") within geographic areas of interest, if such information is not already available in the underlying data base.

Technical Notes

Other kinds of spatial analysis could be done, too, but what we have done here is primarily descriptive and only scratches the surface in terms of what *could* be done by those leaning toward the application of a broader set of spatial statistics.

What follows is a chapter-by-chapter summary of some of the technical aspects of the presentation. This is by no means comprehensive and merely outlines the bare bones of how we did what we did. Explanations tend to get briefer since it is assumed that one explanation of similar products suffices.

Chapter 1

Figure 1.1 was based on data from the National Institute of Justice with updates acquired by searching the World Wide Web. The map was prepared in MapInfo and enhanced slightly in the University of Maryland Baltimore County Cartography Lab.

Figures 1.2 and 1.3 were derived from data in the annual *Sourcebook of Criminal Justice Statistics* and made into graphics using Microsoft Excel.

Chapter 2

As noted in the first part of chapter 2, the analysis involved the somewhat complicated interweaving of three data sets: the Espy File, documented elsewhere in the book, historical statistics for the United States, and vital statistics. The first two were obtained in digital form from ICPSR, while the vital statistics were transcribed from documentary sources. It should be noted here that Espy File data could be spatially enabled owing to the presence in the file of so-called "FIPS" codes identifying states and counties. (FIPS codes are standard codes employed by the federal government in census publications, for example. Any *County and City Data Book*, a census publication, lists FIPS codes for all states, cities, and counties.) Thus, if one has a digital basemap of states and/or counties, the FIPS codes in the basemap file and the data file should match, permitting the joining of the two files in the desktop mapping program ("by" FIPS code), and so allowing the program to assign the data values to their proper spaces on the map(s).

Annual execution frequencies were compiled in SAS for figure 2.1 by simply counting observations by year and creating a new data set in ASCII format that could then be introduced into MapInfo for preparation of the graph. A similar process was used for preparation of the U.S. county maps, figures 2.2–2.5. Subsets of executions were created in order to conform to the temporal boundaries of the eras and then the counting of observations was done by county within each subset, or if necessary, by year (or range of years) and by county (figures 2.6, 2.7).

Figures 2.8 and 2.9 are straightforward MapInfo products using a digital states basemap.

Chapter 4

Note 6 to chapter 4 provides a sketch of correspondence analysis. The concept of inertia as illustrated in table 4.2 is described by Hoffman and Franke (1986, 218–219) as: "the weighted sum of squared distances from the point to their respective centroids, and is equivalent for both sets of points . . . it is because of the geometric correspondence of the two sets of points, in position and inertia, that we can merge the two displays into one joint display. The advantage of this merger is that a concise graphical display representing varied features of the data is obtained in a single picture." For a more in-depth description of correspondence analysis, the Hoffman and Franke article is recommended.

Chapter 5

All 20 graphics (maps and graphs) in chapter 5 were produced in MapInfo with some preliminary processing in SAS in most cases. Figure 5.6 utilized the CD-ROM version of the *Statistical Abstract of the United States*, which permitted saving an ASCII file of county population data by race that could then be introduced into MapInfo. Figure 5.7 involved taking the Espy File and producing a subset such that only persons with race code = 2 (black) were included and then frequency counts were developed by county.

Chapter 6

Technical issues are discussed in full in the chapter. Figure 6.1 was prepared in MapInfo; the county combinations shown were selected from a digital counties basemap. County combinations were selected on the basis of visual inspection of the map of U.S. counties.

Notes

1. SAS Institute, Inc., 100 SAS Campus Drive, Cary, NC 27513-2414.
2. SPSS, Inc., 444 N. Michigan Avenue, Chicago, IL 60611.

3. MapInfo Corporation, One Global View, Troy, NY 12180-8399. Other desktop mapping software (or statistical analysis software) could be used. A popular alternative is ArcView, the Windows version of ARC/INFO, probably the most widely used GIS package.

4. Inter-university Consortium for Political and Social Research, P.O. Box 1248, Ann Arbor, MI 48106.

References

Amnesty International. 1995. Facts and figures on the death penalty. Narrative located at World Wide Web site: www.chem.leeds/ac/uk:80/amnesty/deathp.html.
Amnesty International. 1996. Case of Jesse Jacobs. Narrative located at World Wide Web site: www.derechos.org/amnesty/dp/jessjaco.html.
Anderson, M.L. 1983. *Thinking About Women: Sociological and Feminist Perspectives*. New York: Macmillan.
Archer, D., R. Garner, and M. Beittel. 1983. Homicide and the death penalty: A cross-national test of deterrence hypothesis, *The Journal of Criminal Law and Criminology*. 74:991–1013.
Archer, D. and R. Gartner. 1984. *Violence and Crime in Cross-National Perspective*. New Haven: Yale University Press.
Associated Press. 1996. 56 inmates executed in 1995, most since 1957. *Baltimore Sun*, 2 January, 3A.
Bailey, W.C. 1977. Imprisonment v. the death penalty as a deterrent to murder. *Law and Human Behavior*. 1:239–260.
Bailey, W.C. 1982. Capital punishment and lethal assaults against police *Criminology* 19:608–625.
Bailey, W.C. 1984a. Poverty, Inequality and city homicide rates: some not so unexpected findings. *Criminology* 22:531–550.
Bailey, W.C. 1984b. Murder and capital punishment in the nation's capital. *Justice Quarterly* 1:211–233.
Bailey, W.C. 1991. The general prevention effect of capital punishment for non-capital felonies. In *The Death Penalty in America: Current Research*, Robert M. Bohm, ed. Cincinnati: Anderson Publishing.
Bailey, W.C., and R.D. Peterson. 1990. Capital punishment and non-capital crimes: a test of deterrence, general prevention, and system-overload arguments. *Albany Law Review* 54:681–707.
Bailey, W.C., and R.D. Peterson. 1994. Murder, capital punishment, and deterrence: A review of the evidence and an examination of police killings. *Journal of Social Issues* 50:53–74.
Baker, P. 1994a. Virginia bill would let victims' relatives view executions. *Washington Post*, 1 March, B1, B5.
Baker, P. 1994b. Virginia's execution of double murderer may be last for its electric chair. *Washington Post*, 4 March, D6.
Baker, P. 1995. Virginia has record of 9 executions planned for next 3 months. *Washington Post*, 20 September, B1, B6.
Baker, P., and C. Babington. 1994. Virginia Assembly adds option for execution. *Washington Post*, 26 February, A1, A8.

Baldus, D.C., and J.W.L. Cole. 1975. A comparison of the work of Thorsten Sellin and Isaac Ehrlich on the deterrent effect of capital punishment. *Yale Law Journal* 85:170–186.

Barnett, A. 1981. The deterrent effect of capital punishment: A test of some recent studies. *Operations Research* 29:346–370.

Bedau, H.A. ed. 1982. *The Death Penalty in America*. New York: Oxford University Press.

Bedau, H.A., and C.M. Pierce, eds. 1976. *Capital Punishment in the United States*. New York: AMS Press.

Biskupic, J. 1994. Blackmun turns away from legal "machinery of death." *Washington Post*, 23 February, A1 and A14.

Black, T., and T. Orsagh. 1978. New evidence on the efficacy of sanctions as a deterrent to homicide. *Social Science Quarterly* 58:616–631.

Blacksell, M., C. Watkins, and K. Economides. 1986. Human geography and law: a case of separate development in social science. *Progress in Human Geography* 10:371–396.

Block, C.R. 1986. *Homicide in Chicago*. Chicago: Center for Urban Policy, Loyola University.

Bohm, R.M. 1991a. American death penalty opinion, 1936–1986: A critical examination of the Gallup polls. In *The Death Penalty in America: Current Research*, ed. R.M. Bohm, Chap. 8, 113–145. Cincinnati: Anderson Publishing.

Bohm, R.M. 1991b. *The Death Penalty in America: Current Research*. Cincinnati: Anderson Publishing, vii.

Booth, W. 1994. Florida wants to be on the cutting edge of get-tough crime remedies. *Washington Post*, 17 February, A3.

Bowers, W.J. 1974. *Executions in America*. Lexington, MA: Lexington Books.

Bowers, W.J. 1984. *Legal homicide: Death as punishment in America, 1864–1982*. Boston: Northeastern University Press.

Bowers, W.J. 1988. The effect of executions is brutalization, not deterrence. In *Challenging Capital Punishment: Legal and Social Sciences Approaches*, ed. K.C. Haas and J.A. Inciardi. Newbury Park, CA: Sage.

Bowers, W.J., and G.L. Pierce. 1975. The illusion of deterrence in Isaac Ehrlich's research on capital punishment. *Yale Law Journal* 85:187–208.

Bowers, W.J., and G.L. Pierce. 1980a. Arbitrariness and discrimination under post-Furman capital statutes. *Crime and Delinquency* 26:563–575.

Bowers, W.J. and G.L. Pierce. 1980b. Deterrence or brutalization: What is the effect of executions? *Crime and Delinquency* 26:453–484.

Brearly, H.C. 1932. *Homicide in the United States*. Chapel Hill: University of North Carolina Press.

British Broadcasting Corporation Overseas Service. 1995. Interview in Texas on the capital punishment issue. 10 January.

Buffum, P.C. 1973. Prison killings and death penalty legislation. *Prison Journal* 53:49–57.

Chaiklin, H. and L. Fultz. 1985. The service needs of older offenders. *Justice Professional* 1:26–33.

Chan, P.K.M. 1990. Eighth Amendment—the death penalty and the mentally retarded criminal: Fairness, culpability, and death. *Journal of Criminal Law and Criminology* 80:1211–1235.

Cheatwood, D. and K. Block. 1990. Youth and homicide: an investigation of the age factor in criminal homicide. *Justice Quarterly* 7:265–292.

Cheatwood, D. 1985. Capital punishment and corrections: Is there an impending crisis? *Crime and Delinquency.* 31:461–479.

Cheatwood, D. 1988. Is there a season for homicide? *Criminology* 26:287–306.

Cheatwood, D. 1990. Black homicides in Baltimore 1974–1986: Age, gender, and weapon use changes. *Criminal Justice Review* 15 #2, 1990.

Chressanthis, G. 1989. Capital punishment and the deterrent effect revisited: Recent time series econometric evidence. *Journal of Behavioral Economics* 18:81–97.

Cloninger, D.O. 1977. Deterrence and the death penalty: A cross-sectional analysis. *Journal of Behavioral Economics* 6:87–105.

Cochran, J.K., M.B. Chamlin, and M. Seth. 1994. Deterrence or brutalization? An impact assessment of Oklahoma's return to capital punishment. *Criminology* 32:107–134.

Cohen, R. 1996. The Archbishop is right. *Washington Post*, 26 March, A13.

Cohen, S. 1974. Human warehouses: the future of our prisons? *New Society* November: 407–411.

Cordner, G. 1983. *The Baltimore County Repeat Offender Planning Project: Final Report*. Towson, MD: Baltimore County Executive Office.

Cover, J.P., and P.D. Thistle. 1988. Time series, homicide, and the deterrent effect of capital punishment. *Southern Economic Journal* 54:615–622.

Day, E.L., A.W. Astin, and W.S. Korn. (annual) *The American Freshman*. Los Angeles: University of California Press.

Daly, C.B. 1991 Massachusetts seen near return to death penalty. *Washington Post*, 18 August, A4, A5.

Decker, S.H. and C.W. Kohfeld. 1990. The deterrent effect of capital punishment in the five most active execution states: A time series analysis. *Criminal Justice Review* 15:173–191.

Decker, S. 1993. Exploring victim-offender relationships in homicide: The role of individual and event characteristics. *Justice Quarterly* 10:585–612.

Dewar, H. 1991. Sweeping anti-crime bill passes easily in Senate. *Washington Post*, 12 July, A1, A12.

Dewar, H. 1994. Senate gives up on health care, passes crime bill: $30.2 billion package approved, 51 to 38, despite GOP assault. *Washington Post*, 25 August, A1.

Doleschal, E. 1979. Crime—some popular beliefs. *Crime and Delinquency* 25:1–8.

Eckholm, E. 1995. Studies find death penalty tied to race of the victim. *New York Times*, 24 February, B1, B2.

Economist. 1985. Death penalty back in fashion. 19 January, 294:26, 29.

Economist. 1989. Conduct unbecoming: Civilized societies do not need the death penalty. 6 May, 311:10–11.

Economist. 1988. Capital punishment laid to rest. 11 June, 307:60.

Ehrlich, I. 1975. Deterrence: evidence and inference. *Yale Law Review* 85:209–227.
Erlich, I. 1975. The deterrent effect of capital punishment: A question of life and death. *American Economic Review* 65:397–417.
Ellsworth, P.C. and S.R. Gross. 1994. Hardening of the attitudes: Americans' views on the death penalty. *Journal of Social Issues* 50:19–52.
Espy, M.W., and J.O. Smykla. 1987 *Executions in the United States, 1608–1987: The Espy File*. Machine-readable data file ICPSR 8451. Tuscaloosa, AL: J.O. Smykla, producer. Ann Arbor, MI: Inter-University Consortium for Political and Social Research, distributor.
Felten, E. 1996. The death penalty's glass ceiling. *Wall Street Journal*, 24 January, A13.
Flanagan, T.J. 1980a. The pains of long-term imprisonment: a comparison of British and American perspectives. *British Journal of Criminology* 20:148–156.
Flanagan, T.J. 1980b. Time served and institutional misconduct: patterns of involvement in disciplinary infractions among long-term and short-term inmates. *Journal of Criminal Justice* 8:357–367.
Flanagan, T.J. 1982. Correctional policy and the long-term prisoner. *Crime and Delinquency* 28:82–95.
Foley, L.A., and R.S. Powell. 1982. The discretion of prosecutors, judges, and juries in capital cases. *Criminal Justice Review* 7:16–22.
Forst, B. 1977. The deterrent effect of capital punishment: A cross-state analysis of the 1960s. *Minnesota Law Review* 61:743–767.
Forst, B. 1983. Capital punishment and deterrence: Conflicting evidence? *Journal of Criminal Law and Criminology* 74:927–942.
Fox, J.A. and M.L. Radelet. 1987. Persistent flaws in econometric studies of the deterrent effect of the death penalty. *Loyola of Los Angeles Law Review* 23:29–44.
Freedman, J.L. 1990. The effect of capital punishment on jurors' willingness to convict. *Journal of Applied Social Psychology* 20:465–477.
Furman v. Georgia, 408 U.S. 238 1972.
Gendreau, P. 1988. Capital punishment. *The Canadian Encyclopedia*. Vol. 2. Edmonton: Hurtig Publishers, 360–361.
Gibbs, J.P. 1978. Preventive effects of capital punishment other than deterrence. *Criminal Law Bulletin* 14:34–50.
Gibbs, J.P. 1977. A critique of the scientific literature on capital punishment and deterrence. *Journal of Behavioral Economics* 6:279–309.
Glick, H.R., and G.W. Pruet, Jr. 1985. Crime, public opinion and trial courts: An analysis of sentencing policy. *Justice Quarterly* 2:319–343.
Golden, R.M., and S.F. Messner. 1987. Dimensions of racial inequality and rates of violent crime. *Criminology* 25:525–541.
Goshko, J.M. 1996. Police killing sparks debate on death penalty in New York. *Washington Post*, 24 March, A24.
Greenwood, P. 1982. *Selective Incapacitation*. Santa Monica, CA.: The Rand Corporation.
Gregg v. Georgia, 96 U.S. 2902 1976.

Grogger, J. 1990. The deter-rent effect of capital punishment: An analysis of daily homicide counts. *Journal of the American Statistical Association* 85:295–303.

Gross, S.R., and R. Mauro. 1984. Patterns of death: An analysis of racial disparities in capital sentencing and homicide victimization. *Stanford Law Review* 37:27–153.

Gross, S.R., and R. Mauro. 1989. *Death and Discrimination: Racial Disparities in Capital Sentencing*. Boston: Northeastern University Press.

Haney, C., and D.D. Logan. 1994. Broken promise: The Supreme Court's response to social science research on capital punishment. *Journal of Social Issues* 50:75–101.

Hansen, C. 1969. *Witchcraft at Salem*. New York: G. Braziller.

Harries, K.D. 1971. The geography of American crime. *Journal of Geography*. 70:204–213.

Harries, K.D. 1974. *The Geography of Crime and Justice*. New York: McGraw-Hill.

Harries, K.D. 1985. The historical geography of homicide in the United States, 1935–80, *Geoforum*, 16:73–83.

Harries, K.D. 1988. Regional variations in homicide, capital punishment, and perceived crime severity in the United States. *Geografiska Annaler*, series B. 70:325–334.

Harries, K.D. 1992. Gender, execution, and geography in the United States. *Geografiska Annaler*, series B. 74:21–29.

Harries, K.D. 1995. The last walk: A geography of execution in the United States, 1786–1985. *Political Geography* 14:473–495.

Harries, K.D. 1996. *Serious Violence: Patterns of Homicide and Assault in America*, 2nd ed. Springfield, IL: Charles C. Thomas.

Harries, K.D. and S. Brunn. 1978. *The Geography of Laws and Justice: Spatial Perspectives on the Criminal Justice System*. New York: Praeger.

Harries, K.D. and R.P. Lura. 1974. The geography of justice: Sentencing variations in U.S. judicial districts. *Judicature* 57:392–401.

Harriston, K.A. 1992. A broad death initiative: D.C. law would not exclude juveniles. *Washington Post*, 9 October, D1, D4.

Heine, K. 1991. In Delaware, a choice of noose, needle. *Washington Post*, 18 August, A5.

Hentoff, N., and J. Sands. 1989. A death penalty that singles out Indians. *Washington Post*, 16 October, A19.

Hirschi, T. 1969. *Causes of Delinquency*. Berkeley: University of California Press.

Hoenack, S.A., and W.C. Weiler. 1980. A structural model of murder behavior and the criminal justice system, *American Economic Review* 70:327–341.

Hoffman, D.L., and G.R. Franke. 1986. Correspondence analysis: Graphical representation of categorical data in marketing research. *Journal of Marketing Research* 23:213–227.

Hook, D.D., and L. Kahn. 1989. *Death in the Balance*. Lexington, MA: D.C. Heath.

Huff-Corzine, L., J. Corzine, and D.C. Moore. 1991. Deadly connections: Culture, poverty, and the direction of lethal violence. *Social Forces* 69:715–732.

References

Inter-University Consortium for Political and Social Research, n.d. *Historical, Demographic, Economic, and Social Data: The United States, 1790–1970.* Machine-readable data file ICPSR 0003. Ann Arbor, MI: Inter-University Consortium for Political and Social Research.
Irwin, J. 1980. *Prisons in Turmoil.* Boston: Little, Brown.
Isikoff, M. 1991. House backs expansion of federal death penalty. *Washington Post*, 23 October, A10.
Jacobs, J.B. 1977. *Stateville: The Penitentiary in Mass Society.* Chicago: University of Chicago Press.
Jenkins, K. 1992a. Hill moves to put death penalty to vote in D.C. *Washington Post*, 19 September, A1, A5.
Jenkins, K. 1992b. House votes referendum on D.C. death penalty. *Washington Post*, 25 September, A1, A18.
Jolly, R.W. Jr., and E. Sagarin. 1984. The first eight after Furman: who was executed with the return of the death penalty? *Crime and Delinquency* 30:610–623.
Kamen, A. 1989. Number of executions drops despite forecast: States' social, political cultures seen as key. *Washington Post*, 6 November, A4.
Keil, T.J., and Vito, G.F. 1989. Race, homicide severity, and application of the death penalty: A consideration of the Barnett Scale. *Criminology* 27:511–535.
Keil, T.J., and G.F. Vito. 1991. Kentucky prosecutors' decision to seek the death penalty: A LISREL model. In *The Death Penalty in America: Current Research*, ed. R.M. Bohm, 53–69, Cincinnati: Anderson Publishing.
Keve, P.W. 1992. The costliest punishment: A corrections administrator contemplates the death penalty. *Federal Probation* 4:11–15.
Kleck, G. 1981. Racial discrimination in criminal sentencing: A critical evaluation of the evidence with additional evidence on the death penalty. *American Sociological Review* 46:783–805.
Kowalski, G.S., C.E. Faupel, and P.D. Starr. 1987. Urbanism and suicide: A study of American counties. *Social Forces* 66:85–101.
Kowalski, G.S. and D. Duffield. 1990. The effect of rural population on homicide rates across the rural-urban continuum: A county level analysis *American Journal of Criminal Justice* 15:172–194.
Krahn, H., T.F. Hartnagel, and J.W. Gartrell. 1986. Income inequality and homicide rates: Cross-national data and criminological theories. *Criminology* 24:269–295
LaFree, G., K.A. Drass, and P. O'Day. 1992. Race and crime in postwar America: Determinants of African-American and white rates, 1957–1988. *Criminology* 30:157–188.
Land, K.C., P.L. McCall, and L.E. Cohen. 1990. Structural covariates of homicide rates: Are there any invariances across time and social space? *American Journal of Sociology* 95:922–963.
Lander, B. 1954. *Towards an Understanding of Juvenile Delinquency.* New York: Columbia University Press.
Layson, S.K. 1985. Homicide and deterrence: A reexamination of the United States time-series evidence. *Southern Economic Journal* 52:68–89.

Lempert, R. 1983. The effect of executions on homicides: A new look in an old light. *Crime and Delinquency* 29:88–115.

Lewin, T. 1995. Who decides who will die? Even within states, it varies. *New York Times*, 23 February, A1, B6.

Loftin, C., and R.H. Hill. 1974. Regional subculture and homicide: An examination of the Gastil-Hackney thesis. *American Sociological Review* 39:714–724.

Loftin, C., and R.N. Parker. 1985. An errors-in-variable model of the effect of poverty on urban homicide rates. *Criminology* 23:269–285.

Lottier, S. 1938. Distribution of criminal offenses in sectional regions. *Journal of Criminal Law and Criminology* 29:329–344.

Maguire, K., and T.J. Flanagan. 1991. *Sourcebook of Criminal Justice Statistics—1990*. Washington D.C.: U.S. Department of Justice.

Maguire, K., and A.L. Pastore. 1995. *Sourcebook of Criminal Justice Statistics—1994*. Washington D.C.: Bureau of Justice Statistics.

Margolick, D. 1991. In land of death penalty, accusations of racial bias. *New York Times*, 10 July, A1, A12.

Martin, S. 1983. Commutation of prison sentences: practice, promise, and limitation. *Crime and Delinquency* 29:593–612.

Massey, C.R. and J. McKean. 1985. The social ecology of homicide: A modified lifestyle/routine activities perspective. *Journal of Criminal Justice* 13:417–428.

Masur, L.P. 1989. *Rites of Execution: Capital Punishment and the Transformation of American Culture, 1776–1865*. New York: Oxford University Press.

McCarthy, M. 1983. The health status of elderly inmates. *Corrections Today* 45:64–65, 74.

McFarland, S.G. 1983. Is capital punishment a short-term deterrent to homicide? A study of the effects of four recent American executions. *Journal of Criminal Law and Criminology* 74:1014–1032.

McGahey, R.M. 1980. Dr. Ehrlich's magic bullet: Econometric theory, econometrics, and the death penalty. *Crime and Delinquency* 26:485–502.

Messner, S.F. 1983a. Regional and racial effects on the urban homicide rate: The subculture of violence revisited. *American Journal of Sociology*, 88:997–1007.

Messner, S.F. 1983b. Regional differences in the economic correlates of the urban homicide rate. *Criminology* 21:477–488.

Messner, S.F., and R.J. Sampson. 1991. The sex ratio, family disruption, and rates of violent crime: The paradox of demographic structure. *Social Forces* 69:693–713.

Mills, E.M. 1983. Eighth amendment—cruel and unusual punishment: Habitual offender's life sentence without parole is disproportionate. *Journal of Criminal Law and Criminology* 74:1372–1386.

Morganthau, T., et al. 1995 Condemned to life. *Newsweek*, 7 August, 19–23.

Morton, J. B., and J. C. Anderson. 1982. Elderly offenders: The forgotten minority. *Corrections Today* 44:14–16, 20.

Munford, R. S., R. S. Kazer, R. A. Feldman, and R. R. Stivers. 1976. Homicide trends in Atlanta. *Criminology* 14:213–232.

NAACP (National Association for the Advancement of Colored People) Legal Defense Fund. 1992. *Death Row, U.S.A.*. New York: NAACP Legal Defense and Education Fund.
Nakel, B.O. 1978. The cost of the death penalty. *Criminal Law Bulletin* 14:69–80.
National Center for Health Statistics. Annual. *Vital Statistics of the United States*. Washington, D.C.: U.S. Government Printing Office.
National Institute of Justice. 1986. *Targeting Law Enforcement Resources: The Career Criminal Focus*. Washington, D.C.: U.S. Government Printing Office.
National Institute of Justice. 1981. *Career Criminal Program National Evaluation: Final Report*. Washington, D.C.: U.S. Government Printing Office.
Passell, P. 1975. The deterrent effect of the death penalty: A statistical test. *Stanford Law Review* 28:61–80.
Passell, P., and J. Taylor. 1977. The deterrent effect of capital punishment: Another view. *American Economic Review* 67:445–451.
Paternoster, R. 1991. Prosecutorial discretion and capital sentencing in North and South Carolina. In ed. R.M. Bohm, *The Death Penalty in America: Current Research*, 39–52. Cincinnati: Anderson Publishing.
Perley, S. 1928: *The History of Salem*. Haverhill, MA: Record Publishing.
Petersilia, J., P.M. Greenwood, and M. Lavin. 1978. *Criminal Careers of Habitual Felons*. Washington, D.C.: U.S. Government Printing Office.
Peterson, R.D., and W.C. Bailey. 1991. Felony murder and capital punishment: An examination of the deterrence question, *Criminology* 29:367–395.
Phillips, D.P. 1980. The deterrent effect of capital punishment: new evidence on an old controversy. *American Journal of Sociology* 86:139–148.
Phillips, D.P. 1981. Strong and weak research designs for detecting the impact of capital punishment of homicide. *Rutgers Law Review* 33:790–798.
Pressley, S.A. 1992. A well-traveled walkway to death: Quickened pace of executions leaves its mark on Va.'s 'Row.' *Washington Post*, 2 September, A1, A28.
Pressley, S.A. 1995. Death row and the pace of justice. *Washington Post*, 1 February, A1, A13.
Pressley, S.A. 1996. Execution in Texas: A satisfying end for family of two victims. *Washington Post*, 11 February, A3
Radelet, M.L., H.A. Bedau, and C.E. Putnam. 1994. *In Spite of Innocence: Erroneous Convictions in Capital Cases*. Boston: Northeastern University Press.
Ragland, J. 1991a. Dixon backs look at death penalty: Mayor says choice should be D.C.'s to make. *Washington Post*, 8 August, C1, C2.
Ragland, J. 1991b. D.C. violence revives talk of death penalty: Community leaders cite shifts in attitudes, but few embrace capital punishment. *Washington Post*, 9 August, A16.
Rahiv, G. 1983. Homicide and death penalty: A cross-sectional time series analysis. *International Journal of Comparative and Applied Criminal Justice* 7:61–71.
Rand, M. 1992. Personal communication, Bureau of Justice Statistics, Washington, D.C.

Raspberry, W. 1994. Impossible to be fair. *Washington Post*, 18 March, A22.
Reed, M. B., and F.D. Glasmer. 1979. Aging in a total institution: The case of older prisoners. *The Gerontologist* 19:354–360.
Reidel, M., M.A. Zahn, and L.F. Mock. 1985. *The Nature and Pattern of American Homicide*. Washington: U.S. Department of Justice.
Reuters. 1995. Belgium to strike death penalty from penal statute. Reported 12 December at World Wide Web site: http://www.hooked.net/users/plehner/dp/news/12-12-95.html.
Richardson, R.E.L., and K.D. Harries. 1978. *Oklahoma Felony Sentencing Practices*. Norman, Oklahoma: Oklahoma Center for Criminal Justice.
Rose, H.M., and P.D. McClain. 1990. *Race, Place, and Risk*. Albany: State University of New York Press.
Rosenfeld, R., and S.F. Messner. 1991. The social sources of homicide in different types of societies. *Sociological Forum* 6:51–70.
Sampson, R.J. 1985. Race and criminal violence: A demographically disaggregated analysis of urban homicide. *Crime and Delinquency* 31:47–82.
Sampson, R.J. 1987. Urban black violence: The effect of male joblessness and family disruption. *American Journal of Sociology* 93:348–382.
Sanchez, R. 1995. Political bug bites fewer college freshmen: Annual survey of incoming students shows lowest interest in 29 years. *Washington Post*, 9 January, A5.
SAS (Statistical Analysis System) Institute. 1989. *SAS/STAT User's Guide*, Version 6. 4th ed., Vol. 1, Cary, NC: SAS Institute.
Schneider, V., and J.O. Smykla. 1991. A summary analysis of *Executions in the United States, 1608–1987: The Espy File*. In *The Death Penalty in America: Current Research*, ed. R.M. Bohm, 1–19. Cincinnati: Anderson Publishing.
Schuessler, K.F. 1952. The deterrent influence of the death penalty. *Annals of the American Academy of Political and Social Science* 284:54–62.
Sellin, T. 1959. *The Death Penalty*. Philadelphia: American Law Institute.
Sellin, T., ed. 1967. *Capital Punishment*. New York: Harper & Row.
Shelby, R. 1992. Fighting back in murder city: Why Washington needs my capital punishment legislation. *Washington Post*, 8 March, C5.
Sigler, R., and C. Culliver. 1988. Consequences of the Habitual Offender Act on the costs of operating Alabama's prisons. *Federal Probation* 52:57–64.
Simon, R.J. 1967. *As We Saw the Thirties: Essays on Social and Political Movements of a Decade*. Urbana, IL: University of Illinois Press.
Sorrell, T. 1987. *Moral Theory and Capital Punishment*. Oxford: Blackwell.
Spectacle. 1996. Texas kills an innocent man. Narrative located at World Wide Web site: www.spectacle.org/395/texas.html.
Stack, S. 1987. Publicized executions and homicide, 1950–1980. *American Sociological Review* 52:532–540.
State of Maryland. 1993. *Report of the Governor's Commission on the Death Penalty: An Analysis of Capital Punishment in Maryland: 1978 to 1993*. Annapolis, MD: State of Maryland.
Stewart, J., and P. Lieberman. 1982. What is this new sentence that takes away parole? *Student Lawyer* October:14–17, 39.

References

Sutherland, E.H. 1925. Murder and the death penalty. *Journal of Criminal Law, Criminology, and Police Science* 15:522–529.

Teeters, N.K. and C.J. Zibulka n.d.. *Executions Under State Authority*. Reprinted. 1983. In W.J. Bowers *Legal Homicide: Death as Punishment in America, 1864–1982*. Boston: Northeastern University Press, 395–524.

Thomas, P. 1992. A gun for all seasons: 9mm pistols spawn high-tech violence. *Washington Post*, 29 April, A1, A16.

Thomas, P. 1995. The new face of murder in America. *Washington Post*, 23 October, A1, A4.

Torry, S. 1996. Juggling the issue of representing death-row inmates. *Washington Post*, 5 February, *Washington Business* section, 7.

U.S. Bureau of the Census. 1975. *Historical Statistics of the United States, Colonial Times to 1970*. Bicentennial Edition, Part 2, Washington, D.C.: U.S. Government Printing Office.

U.S. Bureau of the Census. 1983. *County and City Data Book, 1983*. Washington D.C.: U.S. Government Printing Office.

U.S. Bureau of the Census. 1984. *Statistical Abstract of the United States: 1985*. 105th edition. Washington, D.C.: U.S. Government Printing Office.

U.S. Bureau of the Census. 1988. *County and City Data Book, 1989*. Washington, D.C.: U.S. Government Printing Office.

U.S. Bureau of the Census. 1992. *1990 Census of Population and Housing Summary Tape File 1C CD90-1C*. Washington, D.C.: U.S. Government Printing Office.

U.S. Centers for Disease Control. 1986. *Homicide Surveillance: High-Risk Racial and Ethnic Groups—Blacks and Hispanics 1970–1983*. Atlanta: Centers for Disease Control.

U.S. Committee on the Judiciary. 1994. *Racial disparities in Federal death penalty prosecutions, 1988–1994*. Staff Report by the Subcommittee on Civil and Constitutional Rights. 103rd Cong., 2nd. sess.

U.S. Department of Justice. 1985a. *Prison Admissions and Releases, 1982*. Washington, D.C.

U.S. Department of Justice. Bureau of Justice Statistics 1983. *Capital Punishment, 1982*. Washington, D.C.

U.S. Department of Justice. Bureau of Justice Statistics. 1984. *Capital Punishment, 1983*. Washington, D.C.

U.S. Department of Justice. Bureau of Justice Statistics. 1988. *Report to the Nation on Crime and Justice* 2nd edition. Washington, D.C.

U.S. Department of Justice. Bureau of Justice Statistics. 1990. *Capital Punishment, 1989*. Washington, D.C.

U.S. Department of Justice. Bureau of Justice Statistics. 1991a. *Capital Punishment, 1990*. Washington, D.C.

U.S. Department of Justice. Bureau of Justice Statistics. 1991b. *National Update*. Washington, D.C.

U.S. Department of Justice. Federal Bureau of Investigation. 1986. *Uniform Crime Reports, 1985*. Washington, D.C.

U.S. Department of Justice. Federal Bureau of Investigation. 1993. *Uniform Crime Reports, 1993*. Washington, D.C.

U.S. Department of Justice. 1985b. *Sourcebook of Criminal Justice Statistics— 1984*. Washington, D.C.
U.S. Department of Justice. 1986. *Sourcebook of Criminal Justice Statistics— 1985*. Washington, D.C.
U.S. Department of Justice. 1988. *Report to the Nation on Crime and Justice*, 2nd ed. Washington, D.C.
U.S. Department of Justice. 1992. *Capital Punishment in the United States, 1973–1990* [Computer file]. Compiled by U.S. Department of Commerce, Bureau of the Census. First ICPSR ed. Ann Arbor, MI: Inter-University Consortium for Political and Social Research, producer and distributor.
van den Haag, E. and J.P. Conrad. 1983. *The Death Penalty: A Debate*. New York: Plenum Press.
Verhovek, S.H. 1995. Across the U.S., executions are neither swift nor cheap. *New York Times*, 22 February, A1, B2.
Vick, K. 1996a. Delaware readies gallows as rare form of execution draws near. *Washington Post*, 21 January, B1, B4.
Vick, K. 1996b. An execution in the old way: Delaware hanging evokes justice of another era. *Washington Post*, 26 January, B1, B2.
Vold, G.B. 1932. Can the death penalty prevent crime? *Prison Journal* 12:3–8.
Von Drehle, D. 1995a. Cranking up the killing machine. *Washington Post*, 26 February, C1.
Von Drehle, D. 1995b. Miscarriage of justice: Why the death penalty doesn't work. *Washington Post Magazine*, 5 February, 8–13, 20–24.
Von Drehle, D. 1995c. *Among the Lowest of the Dead: The Culture of Death Row*. New York: Random House.
Washington Post. 1991a. In Congress, an outrageous crime bill. Editorial. 26 October, A26.
Washington Post. 1991b. Virginia alters its procedure for executions in electric chair. Editorial. 24 August, B3.
Washington Post. 1995. Execution and inconsistency. Editorial. 4 January, A14.
Whitt, H.P., J. Corzine, and L. Huff-Corzine. 1995. Where is the South? A preliminary analysis of the southern subculture of violence. Trends, risks, and interventions in lethal violence. *Proceedings of the Third Annual Spring Symposium of the Homicide Research Working Group*. Washington D.C.: National Institute of Justice, 127–148.
Wilgoren, D. 1992. Carjackers put drivers on defensive: taking vehicles by force has led to 5 area deaths this year. *Washington Post*, 16 August, A1, A16.
Will, G. 1994 Justice Blackmun's Outburst. *Washington Post*, 27 February, C7.
Wilson, D.G., and G.F. Vito. 1986. *Imprisoned Elders: The Experience of One Institution*. Paper presented at National Meeting of the Academy of Criminal Justice Sciences, Las Vegas.
Wolfgang, M.E. 1978. The death penalty: Social philosophy and social science research. *Criminal Law Bulletin* 14:18–33.
Wolfgang, M.E., R.M. Figlio, P.E. Tracy, and S.I. Singer. 1985. *The National Survey of Crime Severity*. Washington, D.C.: U.S. Department of Justice, Bureau of Justice Statistics.

References

Wolfgang, M.E., R.M. Figlio, and T. Sellin. 1972. *Delinquency in a Birth Cohort*. Chicago: University of Chicago Press.

Wright, J.H. 1990. Life-Without-Parole: An alternative to death or not much of a life at all. *Vanderbilt Law Review* 43:529–568.

Wright, J.H. 1991. Life-Without-Parole: The view from death row. *Criminal Law Bulletin* 27:334–357.

Yang, J.E. 1991. Bush anti-crime speech echoes 1988 campaign. *Washington Post*, 15 August, A8.

Yunker, J.A. 1982. Testing the deterrent effect of capital punishment: A reduced form approach. *Criminology* 19:626–649.

Yunker, J.A. 1983. The relevance of the identification problem to statistical research on capital punishment. *Crime and Delinquency* 28:96–124.

Zimring, F.E., and G. Hawkins. 1986. *Capital Punishment and the American Agenda*. Cambridge: Cambridge University Press.

INDEX

African-Americans, 18, 36–38, 67, 69, 72, 75, 76, 84, 90, 91, 123

backlog, 6

capital cases, 116; discretion in, 116
capital offender life-without-parole statutes, 111; aggravating or mitigating circumstances, 112; commutation, 114; executive clemency, 114; impact on corrections and prosecution systems, 115; Montana, 112; moral entrepreneurs, 113; Nevada, 112; Washington state, 114; West Virginia, 112
capital punishment, 68, 95, 123; brutalization effect, 96; deterrent effect, 95; free legal counsel, 124; geographic research, 123; Huntsville, Texas, 125; involvement of youthful minorities in violence, 69; longitudinal studies, 96; move to hasten executions, 124; New York City, 124; vengeance as policy rationale, 125; witnesses to executions, 125
capital punishment and geography, 12; death penalty, cultural rootedness of, 13; Florida, 13; *Furman v. Georgia*, 13; Maryland, 13–14; Potomac River, 13; United States, 13; U.S. Supreme Court, 13; Virginia, 13–14; Washington, D.C., 13–14
capital punishment and race, 72; California, 72; county-based geography, 75; excessive execution rates, 76; Florida, 72; Georgia, 72; juvenilization" of violence, 76; Kentucky, 72; New York, 72; Ohio, 72; pattern of discrimination, 72; Pennsylvania, 72; rates for African-Americans, 72; rates for whites, 72; South Carolina, 72; Texas, 72; Virginia, 72
corrections, 41; alternatives to capital punishment, 43; "big three" execution states, 46; California, 55; death penalty commitments, 44; deterrence, 42; difficulties in making projections, 45; execution levels, 41; executioners, mental health of, 47; Florence, Colorado, 54; *Furman*, impact of, 50; impending crisis in, 41; increasing death row populations, 57; increasing numbers of inmates, 44; life-without-parole, 43, 49, 52, 54; life-without-parole, and costs, 54; life-without-parole,

Index

problems with, 52; Marion, Illinois, 54; possible backlash against capital punishment, 48; possible release of large numbers of inmates, 49; prison population ecology, impact of, 50; prisoner input and output, 51; projections of commitments, 44; public opinion, 41; public opinion, backlash in, 43; rate of executions, 42; rates of execution in Western European nations, 47; segregated areas, 51

correspondence analysis, 64, 66; African-Americans, observed frequency of, 67; chi-square values, 66; homicide region space, 64; inertia in, 65; principal components analysis, 65; as a type of exploratory data analysis, 65

cost of capital punishment, 6; Blackmun, Justice, 6; California, 6; Florida, 6; life imprisonment, 6; New York state, 6; Texas, 6

counties, 97; advantage as units of analysis, 98; analysis of, and NAACP Legal Defense Fund, 104; Benton county, Mississippi, 101; capital punishment variables, 105; Cheshire county, New Hampshire, 100; comparability problem, 97–98; Cowley county, Kansas, 101; criterion for selection, 98; deterrence, 108; displacement, 101, 108; female headed households, 108; Franklin county, Massachusetts, 100; Geneva county, Alabama, 101, 106; geographic factors, 101; Grant county, Oklahoma, 100; Hardeman county, Tennessee, 101; Holmes county, Florida, 101, 106; Kay county, Oklahoma, 100, 101; key variables in analysis, 102; Loudoun county, Virginia, 101; Lyon county, Iowa, 100; Montgomery county, Maryland, 101; multiple regressions, 104; multivariate analyses, 104; Nobles county, Minnesota, 100; Osceola county, Iowa, 100; statistical variation accounted for, 107; Sumner county, Kansas, 100; Uniform Crime Reports, 102; Windham county, Vermont, 100

county-based analysis, 94; contiguity, 94; deterrence of violence, 95; matching of counties, 94; sample size, 94

cultural linkage, 119; life-without-parole, 119

data sources, 17; census data, 18; census of population, 18; death penalty, 127; Espy File, 17; Espy, M. Watt, 17; executions, 17; first recorded execution, 17; historical, demographic, economic, and social data, 18; Inter-University Consortium for Political and Social Research, 18; moral authority, 126; vital statistics of the United States, 18

death penalty approval, 7; changes in public approval of

capital punishment, 10; college freshmen, 7; Furman case, 7; Indiana, 9; McVeigh, Timothy, 9; Newsweek opinion poll data, 9; Oklahoma City Federal Building bombing case, 9; place-to-place variation in execution, 10; police chiefs' opinions, 8; polls, 7; Roper poll, 8; Smith, Susan, case, 9

death row population, 88; African-Americans, 90; Anti-Drug Abuse Act of 1988, 91; federal capital sentencing, 91; female juveniles, 88; mentally handicapped, 91; non-murder offenses, 90; racial bias, 91; women, 88

directions, 14; costs of capital punishment, 15; data, visualization of, 15; error in capital punishment, 15; Espy File, 14; Headland, Alabama, 14; Inter-University Consortium for Political and Social Research, 14; social science analysis, 14; spatio-temporal view, 15

execution experience since 1987, 30; Florida, 31; recent executions, trend in, 31; Texas, 31; Virginia, 31

execution, geography of, 63; Georgia, 63; intrastate variations in, 63; North Florida, 63; regional cultures of, 63; South Florida, 63; systematic variations in, 63

execution, methods of, 24; Arizona, 25; California, 25; Colorado, 25; Delaware, 28; electrocution, 24; firing squad, 28; gas chamber, 25; hanging, 28; humaneness of, 25; lethal injection, 25; Missouri, 25; Nevada, 25; New York state, 25; North Carolina, 25; Ohio, 25; Oklahoma, 25; Oregon, 25; origin and diffusion, 24; other methods, 27; Texas, 25; U.S. Army, 28; Utah, 29; Wyoming, 25

execution rates and homicide rates, relationships between, 65; regression residuals, 66

execution, recent trends, 29; crack cocaine culture, 29; death belt, 30; *Furman v. Georgia*, 30; hypotheses, 30; Miami, Florida, 29; retribution, 30; southern emphasis, 30; Texas, 30; violent crime, new forms of, 29; Virginia, 30; weapons, 29

gender, 84; attribute comparisons, 84; comparative severity weighting, 86; crime categories, 85; method of execution, 86; occupation, 85

gender disparity in capital punishment, 92; battered spouse syndrome, 92

geographic variation, 126; persistence of, 126

homicide and execution: average time from conviction to execution, 33; *Foreman v. Georgia*, 34; homicides, and execution production, 33; longitudinal data, 34; mean execution rate, 33;

standardized rates, 32; states with historically high rates, 34; twentieth-century trends, 34
homicide rates, 69; discrimination, 69; high execution rates, 69

international perspectives: Amnesty International, 2; Belgium, 1; Britain, 1; Canada, 1; China, 1–2; Eastern Europe, 2; European Human Rights Convention, 2; Germany, 2; Hungary, 2; Iran, 1–2; Nigeria, 1–2; Soviet Union, 2

life-without-parole laws, 121; geographic distribution of, 121
life-without-parole sentence, 109; as alternative to a death sentence, 109; difference from normal life sentence, 109; elderly inmate population, 118; impact of, 109; impact on the correctional system, 116; Marion, Illinois, federal penitentiary, 117; security issues, 117; Stateville, Illinois, penitentiary, 117

Maryland, 35; African-Americans, more likely to be executed, 36; *Furman v. Georgia*, 36; Murdy Committee on Capital Punishment, 35; new statute, 1978, 36; perceived unfairness of the death penalty, 36; Report of the Governor's Commission on the Death Penalty, 36; suburban counties, 36; urbanized areas, 36

opinion polls, 7; Gallup poll, 7; gender, 7; politics, 7; race, 7; region, 7; socioeconomic status, 7

persons executed, attributes of, 18; African-Americans, 18; age, 18; American Civil War, 23; American Revolution, 23; assassinations, 24; burglary-murder, 19; car-jacking, 4; choropleth maps, 20; county geography, 20; decline era, 19; dichotomy, in execution convictions, 22; District of Columbia, 4; drive-by shootings, 4; Fairness in Death Sentencing Act, 3; *Furman v. Georgia*, 24; Great Depression, 24; growth era, 19; male, 18; murder, 19; national patterns, 19; New Deal, 24; occupational structure, 18; Oklahoma, 22; peak era, 19; Pennsylvania, 22; political pressure, 3; Prohibition, 24; public opinion, 23; rape-murder, 19; slaves, 19; South, 22; stability era, 19; U.S. Congress, 3–4; U.S. Senate, 3; Virginia, 22
proportionality of punishment, 71

regional and local culture, 34; Dallas, Texas, 35; death belts, 35; Georgia, 35; Houston, Texas, 35; New Mexico, 34; New York state, 35;

prosecutorial discretion, 35;
Simpson, O.J., case, 35;
Smith, Susan, case, 35;
Tennessee, 35; Texas, 34

Shelby, Senator Richard,
initiative, 4; Barnes, Tom, 4;
Contract with America, 5;
House of Representatives, 4;
Washington, D.C., death
penalty in, 4

theory and deterrence, 10–11

United States, 2, 123; death row,
3; *Furman v. Georgia*, 2; high
rates of violent crime, 123;
number of prisoners under
sentence of death, 2; prisoners
executed in 1995, 3

values, 11; deterrence
hypothesis, rejection of, 11;
homicide, background rate,
12; homicide, factors causing
changes in, 12
violence: capital punishment
eras, 62; Crime Control Act of
1993, 60; federal death
penalties, 60; *Furman v.
Georgia*, 61; National Survey
of Crime Severity, 61; Nevada,
62; regional cultures of crime
control, 61; regional patterns
of, 60; regions, 62; southern
violence construct, 61
Virginia, 36; efficiency in
executions, 37; expeditious
review process, 37; low
reversal rate, 37; popular
election of judges, 37;
simplicity of sentencing
procedure, 37

Washington, D.C., 4–5, 37; death
penalty, resistance to, 37;
spying and espionage, 37
women and capital punishment,
76; Essex County,
Massachusetts, 81; execution
of women, 71; Massachusetts,
79; number under sentence of
death, 78; operating
hypothesis, 78; phases of
analysis, 79; regional
distribution, 79; risk of
execution, 81; Salem witch
trials, 81; temporal
framework for analysis, 78;
Virginia, 79
World Wide Web, 71

X model, 38

About the Authors

Keith Harries has been professor of geography at the University of Maryland, Baltimore County, since 1985. His Ph.D. was obtained at UCLA in 1969, where he initially specialized in urban geography. He has worked on criminal justice issues since 1970; his first book was *The Geography of Crime and Justice* (1974), followed by *The Geography of Laws and the Administration of Justice* (1978), *Crime and the Environment* (1980), *Crime: A Spatial Perspective* (1980), *Geographic Factors in Policing* (1990), and *Serious Violence: Patterns of Homicide and Assault in America* (1990, 1996), and other books dealing with geographic themes. His articles have appeared in the *Annals, Association of American Geographers, Criminology, Political Geography, Social Indicators Research, Indian Journal of Criminology, Environment and Behavior,* and elsewhere.

He is a member of the Association of American Geographers, the American Society of Criminology, and the Homicide Research Working Group. He serves on the editorial boards of the *Journal of Quantitative Criminology* and *Studies in Crime and Crime Prevention* (Stockholm). As a result of a lecture tour in India, Thailand, and Australia in 1995, his current research includes comparative analysis of homicide patterns in India and the United States in collaboration with the University of Madras, as well as ongoing intraurban analyses of crime patterns utilizing geographic information systems (GIS) methods.

Derral Cheatwood is currently professor of criminal justice and sociology and director of the Division of Social and Policy Sciences at the University of Texas at San Antonio. He obtained his Ph.D. in sociology from Ohio State University in 1972, and his first research dealt primarily with juvenile delinquency and the sociology of visual media. Current research focuses on homicide and corrections, and recent articles have appeared in *Criminology, Justice Quarterly,* the *Journal of Quantitative Criminology, Criminal Justice Review,* the *Journal of Crime and Justice,* and the *European Journal of Crime, Criminal Law, and Criminal Justice*. He is a member of the American Society of Criminology, the Academy of Criminal Justice Sciences, the American Correctional Association, and serves on the Steering Committee of the Homicide Research Working Group.

In 1993 he held a Fulbright Fellowship to the Max Planck Institute for Foreign and International Criminal Law in Freiburg, Germany, and continues to analyze the comparative homicide data gathered there. He has received grants from the National Institute of Corrections, the National Endowment for the Humanities, the National Endowment for the Arts, and a number of state and local agencies. He has also served as a consultant to a variety of local, state, and federal organizations. At present he is involved in gang research and in analysis of data on homicides in the city of San Antonio.

364.6609 Harries, Keith D.
H
The geography of execution.

PAPER BINDER

DATE			

HICKSVILLE PUBLIC LIBRARY
169 JERUSALEM AVE.
HICKSVILLE, N.Y.

BAKER & TAYLOR